# CAMPUSES
## OF CONSENT

# CAMPUSES OF CONSENT

## SEXUAL AND SOCIAL JUSTICE IN HIGHER EDUCATION

THERESA A. KULBAGA

LELAND G. SPENCER

UNIVERSITY OF MASSACHUSETTS

*Amherst & Boston*

ISBN 978-1-62534-459-5 (paper); 458-8 (hardcover)

Designed by Frank Gutbrod
Set in Minion
Printed and bound by Maple Press, Inc.

Cover design by Patricia Duque Campos
Library of Congress Cataloging-in-Publication Data

Names: Kulbaga, Theresa A., author. | Spencer, Leland G., author.
Title: Campuses of consent : sexual and social justice in higher education /
Theresa A. Kulbaga, Leland G. Spencer.
Description: Amherst : University of Massachusetts [2019] |
Includes bibliographical references and index. |

Summary: "This new book for scholars and university administrators offers a provocative critique of sexual justice language and policy in higher education around the concept of consent. Complicating the idea that consent is plain common sense, Campuses of Consent shows how normative and inaccurate concepts about gender, gender identity, and sexuality erase queer or trans students' experiences and perpetuate narrow, regressive gender norms and individualist frameworks for understanding violence. Theresa A. Kulbaga and Leland G. Spencer prove that consent in higher education cannot be meaningfully separated from larger issues of institutional and structural power and oppression. While sexual assault advocacy campaigns, such as It's On Us, federal legislation from Title IX to the Clery Act, and more recent affirmative-consent measures tend to construct consent in individualist terms, as something "given" or "received" by individuals, the authors imagine consent as something that can be constructed systemically and institutionally: in classrooms, campus communication, and shared campus spaces"—Provided by publisher.

Identifiers: LCCN 2019019873 | ISBN 9781625344588 (hardcover) | ISBN
9781625344595 (paperback) | ISBN 9781613767030 (ebook) | ISBN
9781613767023 (ebook)
Subjects: LCSH: Social justice and education—United States. | Sexual
consent—United States. | Sexual harassment in universities and
colleges—United States—Prevention. | Rape in universities and
colleges—United States—Prevention. | Higher education and state. |
Universities and colleges—Social aspects—United States.
Classification: LCC LC192.2 .K85 2019 | DDC 371.7/86—dc23
LC record available at https://lccn.loc.gov/2019019873

British Library Cataloguing-in-Publication Data
A catalog record for this book is available from the British Library

Chapter 4 was previously published as "Trigger warnings as respect for student boundaries in university classrooms" by Leland G. Spencer & Theresa A. Kulbaga (2018), *Journal of Curriculum and Pedagogy*, 15 (1): 106–22, https://doi.org/10.1080/15505170.2018.1438936, reprinted by permission of the publisher (Taylor & Francis Ltd, http://www.tandfonline.com).

# CONTENTS

# ACKNOWLEDGMENTS

This book is the result of years of thinking, reading, and advocating together for more just campuses. We contributed equally to the project, and our names appear in alphabetical order. Institutional critique, and feminist social change more generally, is challenging work. It is also by necessity collaborative work, and we have certainly not been alone in it. We would like to thank our students and colleagues at Miami University who have joined us in analyzing the problems of the neoliberal university and its approach to sexual justice, as well as in offering suggestions for how to do better. Several Miami University offices supported our work: the Office for the Advancement of Research and Scholarship offered funding, as did the Hamilton Campus Research Fund, the College of Liberal Arts and Applied Science, the Department of Interdisciplinary and Communication Studies, and the Department of Literatures, Languages, and Writing.

We thank the professional advocates at Women Helping Women and YWCA Hamilton, especially Kendra Massey and Susan Pelle, who not only shared their knowledge and expertise with us but who also work every day in hospitals, court rooms, police departments, and schools—including our own university—to support survivors of gender-based violence and to educate the wider community about consent.

Theresa especially thanks her students and colleagues in Women's, Gender & Sexuality Studies and her students in Creative Nonfiction Writing, who are a continuous source of inspiration and ideas. I learn so much from you every time I walk into a classroom. Special thanks to the scholars and attendees at the "#Me Too and Epistemic Injustice" conference at CUNY Graduate Center, New York City, October 4–6, 2018, for sharing their work on sexual (in)justice, especially Linda Martín Alcoff, Ann Cahill, Leigh Gilmore, Mishuana Goeman, Kim Hall, Kate Manne, and Gaile Pohlhaus Jr. Parts of chapter 5 were presented at the 2018 National Women's Studies Association conference in Atlanta, GA. Extra-special thanks to Leigh Gilmore for her talk "Graphic Witness: Evidence and Testimony in the #MeToo Movement" and to the participants in the 2018–2019 John W. Altman Program in the Humanities on "Truth and Lies" through Miami University's Humanities Center, who provided the necessary intellectual community to foster many of these ideas. I owe a lifetime of thanks to my mentor and coauthor Wendy S. Hesford for insights about feminism, academia, and institutional critique. I'd also like to thank the following friends and colleagues who have offered conversation, ideas, feedback, brunch, gin and tonics, hikes in the woods with our dogs, pub trivia, glamping trips, music playlists, and countless other forms of support and inspiration: Julie Avril Minich, Susan Pelle, Melissa Spencer, Jennifer Junker, Jason Palmeri, Anita Mannur, Gaile Pohlhaus Jr., Madelyn Detloff, Mary Jean Corbett, Emily Zakin, Katie Kickel, and Chelsea Voulgares.

For daily cuddles and hikes (as well as riveting, if one-sided, conversation), I thank my dog Willa. For joining me in writing this book—as well as being an all-around excellent friend and colleague, not to mention a first-rate wielder of outraged adjectives—I thank Leland G. Spencer with all my heart and mind. Finally—for a lifetime of feminist inspiration, love, and strength—I thank my mother, Barbara Kulbaga, to whom I dedicate this book.

Leland thanks Miami University's Committee on Faculty Research for a summer research appointment in 2017. Audiences at several academic conferences offered helpful feedback: chapter 1 was presented at the 2017 meeting of the National Communication Association in Dallas, Texas, and at a meeting of the masculinities research group at Miami University; chapter 3 began as a presentation to a vice president's panel at the Organization for the Study of Communication, Language, and Gender in Bowling Green, Kentucky, in 2015. I thank Chad McBride for the invitation to participate in the panel and think about these important ideas. Chapter 4 was presented at the 2018 meeting of the Southern States Communication Association in Nashville, Tennessee. Carol Winkelmann's Gender, Religion, and Violence class at Xavier University and Matt Jones's Introduction to Women's, Gender, and Sexuality Studies class at Miami University asked provocative questions, as did several sections of my own Introduction to LGBT Studies classes at Miami.

Thanks to Joshua Trey Barnett for hosting a writing retreat that provided valuable space for thinking and drafting, and for years of sharing friendship and intellectualism. Collaborating with Theresa Kulbaga has been an absolute joy. I have appreciated our warm camaraderie and all the ways Theresa has inspired a deepening of my thinking and a sharpening of my writing. I also acknowledge with gratitude the many colleagues, friends, and family members who have listened to me talk about these ideas for more than two years, especially Jason Rutledge, whose love and patience I cherish daily.

# CAMPUSES
## OF CONSENT

---

# WHAT CAN CONSENT MEAN ON CAMPUS?

I n 2015 the sexual assault awareness and prevention campaign It's On Us produced a public service announcement (PSA) video titled "One Thing." In the video, numerous celebrities argue that consent is "the one thing you can't have sex without. . . . Without it, it's not sex. It's rape" (It's On Us 2018). The PSA argues that consent is central to healthy relationships: "If you don't get it, you don't get it." However, in the video consent is not defined; instead, the PSA ends by referring viewers to the It's On Us website, where they can "learn more" and "take the pledge" to obtain consent.[1] Assuming a self-evident (and individualist) definition of consent, the PSA (and the It's On Us campaign more generally) encourages viewers to "get it"—both to understand consent and to secure it. But we must ask, as we do throughout this book: How is consent defined, and by whom? How is it constructed? Who has it and who has to "get" it? What social and cultural contexts of power and oppression enable or constrain consent? What are the limits of individualist understandings of consent (and of violence) as "one thing"? And finally—beyond our commonsense, normative, or singular concepts—*what can consent mean?*

This book was drafted between 2016 and 2018, years that raised key questions about the meaning(s) of consent, violence, and power. Spring 2016 saw the widely publicized trial and lenient sentencing of rapist and Stanford student Brock Turner, whose victim powerfully

1

spoke out about the trauma she experienced and the importance of cultivating cultures and campuses of consent. In summer, a letter from the dean of students at the University of Chicago went viral. The letter welcomed new first-year students to the university and told them not to expect "trigger warnings" in any of their classes because the university values "freedom of expression"; students' freedom from trauma—their right to emotional and intellectual consent in education—did not register. On our own campus in Ohio, fall semester began with three incidents of reported sexual assault in the first three weeks. Adding to this violence, the campus-wide notices about these crimes offered vague or inaccurate language about consent and implicitly suggested that the victims would not have been assaulted had they not been drinking. In September, Netflix released the documentary film *Audre & Daisy* (2016), which joined *The Invisible War* (2012) and *The Hunting Ground* (2015) in drawing public attention to rape culture on campuses and in the U.S. military. October saw the release of tapes in which U.S. presidential candidate Donald Trump bragged about his ability to "grab 'em [women] by the pussy" without consent; in November, he was elected president. And in December, in the name of "free speech," the University of Wisconsin–Milwaukee invited known transphobic hatemonger and White supremacist Milo Yiannopoulos to speak on campus. During his lecture, he projected photographs of a transgender student, deadnamed her, deliberately used the wrong pronouns, and said "I'd almost still bang him [*sic*]." The targeted student wrote a scathing email to the university and withdrew.

In 2017 and 2018, issues of consent and violence became only more poignant in the wake of Trump's inauguration,[2] the resurgence of the Me Too movement,[3] and the widely publicized testimony of Dr. Christine Blasey Ford against Supreme Court justice nominee Brett Kavanaugh. Given this context, we believe it imperative to rethink consent on college campuses and in the culture at large. In this book, we argue that consent is a useful concept in and beyond interpersonal relationships. We define consent in higher education as *radical respect for physical, intellectual, and emotional boundaries*. On one level, this definition is simple: respect others' boundaries. Period. The simplicity can be evident in individual situations of (for example) sexual consent, in which everyone engaged in sexual activity expresses conscious and enthusiastic assent to continuing participation, and everyone stops if someone says no. Consent is, in straightforward language, respect for boundaries—and this is the case despite a kind of purposeful ambiguity around what consent means that contributes to rape culture. But we also acknowledge what Leland Spencer (2015b) calls the necessity and impossibility of definition. We must define it, particularly given the expressed lack of respect for the boundaries of women, queer and trans students, and other populations statistically vulnerable to disrespect in all its forms. The more we theorize it, the more complex and valenced it becomes. As Laker and Boas (2017) put it on *Consent Stories*, a sister website for their research program "Sexual Coercion and Violence in College":

> We believe that consent is a term that "feels" defined, but it quickly falls apart when we begin to unpack what it actually involves in lived experience. Also, consent is not a static moment, but rather a dynamic decision state that ebbs and flows depending on many variables over time. Coercive forces such as loaded or sexually charged contexts, guilt, shame, anxiety, fear, sexism, homophobia, racism and other forms of bigotry and discrimination, threats of rejection, emotional manipulation and eagerness to please others, all have the possibility of compromising the ideal of a truly consensual experience.

Like Laker and Boas, we are interested in productively problematizing the idea that consent is plain common sense, especially given the ways in which the rhetoric of "common sense" can be used to discredit the need for research and policy. As is so often the case when appeals to common sense are used, normative and inaccurate concepts flow in to fill the cracks left by the lack of a clear definition. And normative and inaccurate concepts, as we show in this book, are part of the problem, especially when they erase queer or trans students' experiences or perpetuate narrow, regressive gender norms and individualist frameworks for understanding violence.

Accordingly, we are not interested in reproducing or exacerbating cultural panic about "hookup culture," Tinder, sexting, leggings, Instagram, selfies, or anything judgement-laden about young people's sexual agency more generally—a kind of panic that, in our view, contributes to victim blaming and results in regressive, paternalistic policies aimed at controlling young women's sexual decisions and self-representation (Hasinoff 2015). Likewise, we follow Native theorist and activist Sarah Deer (2015) in rejecting the "crisis" and "epidemic" rhetoric that treats violence as individual, aberrant, and rare and that constructs women as vulnerable to the extent that they put themselves at risk. While sexual violence is endemic, it is not the result of victims' "risky" behavior, but instead it is the result of oppressive cultural norms that determine whose behavior counts as "risky"—and whose violence is excused and normalized—in the first place.

Following decades of work by feminist and antiracist theorists, we argue that consent in higher education cannot be meaningfully separated from larger issues of institutional and structural power and oppression. When those with power and privilege on campus discredit accusations of violence or harassment, or rationalize it as "normal" gendered behavior, they erode students' understanding of consent and discourage students from "getting it." Moreover, when we say that consent is about respecting boundaries, we understand boundaries to be socially constructed rather than rigid, fixed, or essential. Nor is the individual body a fixed or "immutable, bounded entity" (Barnett 2015, 165). Instead, as shown by foundational work in queer and trans studies, we insist that bodies and boundaries are constructed and that consent is creative and dynamic, as much about letting others "in" as keeping them "out" (as is the case in BDSM practices, for example) (Bauer 2014). Moreover, following scholars in precarity studies, we acknowledge what Wendy S. Hesford, Adela C. Licona, and Christa Teston (2018) call "the affective, relational, and material conditions and structuring logics of inequality" that make campuses dangerous and violent for some (2). Crucially, we insist that consent is an agentic act of acknowledging one's own and another's humanity, and cannot coexist with violence, coercion, or oppression in any form.[4] To say that consent cannot coexist with violence does not mean that it is the same as nonviolence (though nonconsent is one form that violence can take). But while nonconsent is violence, and while our concept of consent considers how it is constructed or constrained by cultural and institutional norms and forms of power, consent by itself is not necessarily sufficient to cultivate nonviolent and just campuses. In other words, consent is *necessary* but not *sufficient* in antiviolence and social justice work.

On campus, our more expansive definition of consent means that we must do more than work to prevent sexual assault; we must radically rethink consent to encompass respect for the whole person—body, mind, emotion, and spirit—and for the campus community at large. While sexual assault advocacy campaigns (such as It's On Us) and even affirmative-consent measures (such as California's "Yes Means Yes" law, SB 967 passed in 2014) often construct consent in individualist terms, as something "given" or "gotten" by individuals, we imagine consent as something possible to construct systemically and institutionally: in classrooms, campus communication, and shared campus spaces. What constructing such spaces entails is the subject of this book.

## CAMPUSES OF NONCONSENT

Regrettably, many colleges and universities function as campuses of nonconsent. By *campuses of nonconsent*, we mean not just that sexual assault is rampant, often unaddressed, and frequently misunderstood, but also that as educational institutions, campuses replicate the power dynamics and structural oppression of the culture at large, which often fails to respect, value, and validate the experiences of women, queer and trans students, students of color, immigrants and refugees, and other oppressed and marginalized populations. Though public awareness and advocacy surrounding rape culture and sexual assault often focus on White, middle-class women, it is important to understand that sexual assault is a tactic used in war, colonialism, slavery, genocide, the military, marriage, and other oppressive structures—including, we argue, college campuses—*as a tool of oppression* (Agosín 2002; Deer 2015; Enloe 2004; Pérez 2008). From this standpoint, a narrow focus on sexual consent and individual bodily autonomy (especially on those with certain bodies or normative gender identities) falls short.

Our premise throughout this book draws on a more capacious understanding of consent than one that focuses exclusively on sexual assault. Without in any way minimizing the significance of sexual consent, we show how the structural logics of nonconsent that underlie rape culture also inform the messages we send and receive about physical consent (even in banal forms like viral memes) and attitudes toward emotional and intellectual consent, such as debates about trigger warnings and the pedagogical practices that can create or challenge epistemic injustice. To be clear: we do not equate rape with bigotry, hate speech, bad teaching, or distasteful memes. Our goal is not to flatten the differences among physical, emotional, and intellectual consent. Instead, we recognize that rape culture is *a culture*, and is enabled and supported by a system of language, practices, social norms, and policies that make violence both possible and common on campus. Theorizing consent as inseparable from power and oppression, this book makes connections among seemingly disparate debates and occurrences, such as students' health and safety, academic freedom, online harassment and hate speech, disability and accessibility, trigger warnings, and teaching practices. What unites each of these issues is the question of *who has the power to be protected from violation*: for example, defending Yiannopoulos's right to "free speech," rather than trans students' right to freedom *from* epistemic violence, is one way that campuses privilege cisnormativity and silence trans and gender-nonconforming students. Philosopher Kate Manne (2018) has usefully coined the term *himpathy* to name the ways in which misogyny aligns empathy with powerful, often White, men and against victims when the latter tell stories about experiencing violence. We can see himpathy at work in the judge's worry for Brock Turner's bright future (and interest in his past swim record), and we observe it in the claim that Yiannopoulos deserves protection and the benefit of the doubt while the student he humiliates does not. In other words, himpathy is one way that privilege and power replicate the status quo and fail to do justice to victim's experiences and narratives.

Of course, rape culture is a key component of cultures and campuses of nonconsent. We use the term *rape culture* to refer to the constitutive practices that normalize and excuse sexual violence, including everything from rape jokes to victim blaming in the aftermath of a reported assault. Campuses exacerbate rape culture when they over-emphasize victims' choices (such as alcohol use, social activities, or time of night) in their messaging, when they permit fraternities to chant "no means yes, yes means anal," and when they spend more energy warning some students how *not* to get raped than teaching all students about what consent means, how it can be cultivated, and why it matters. Mainstream culture, including news media, perpetuates rape culture when it frames allegations of sexual assault as affronts to an athlete's future or when it construes victims as attention mongering or opportunist.[5]

Such an environment cultivates conditions for nonconsent, including sexual assault. While sexual violence is not the only form of nonconsent addressed in this book, it is staggeringly prevalent. Sexual assault affects 1 in 5 women students, by the most conservative estimate, and 1 in 16 men students (National Sexual Violence Resource Center [NSVRC] 2015); women between 18 and 24 experience the highest rate of sexual assault, and college women age 18 to 24 are three times more likely than women in general to experience sexual violence (Rape, Abuse, and Incest National Network [RAINN] 2018). Students almost never (90 percent) choose to report sexual assault (NSVRC 2015).[6] When they do, however, they frequently confront disbelief or blame, especially when they were drinking or on a date, or when the perpetrator is an athlete. Campuses cultivate attitudes, whether overt or implied, that both blame women for assaults and erase men and trans or gender-nonconforming students' experiences of sexual assault. One study found that 24.1 percent of trans, queer, and gender-nonconforming students and 23.1 percent of cisgender women on college campuses experience sexual assault, but only 5.4 percent of cisgender men (Association of American Universities [AAU] 2015). As we noted above, the ubiquity of sexual violence on college campuses has captured popular attention and even amendments to federal legislation (such as Title IX and the Violence Against Women Act); however, what remains invisible are the experiences of students who do not fit narrow, normative constructions of "good" victims and "deserving" subjects.

Addressing the problem of nonconsent on campus means addressing the interlocking structures of oppression that empower the privileged and disempower the oppressed. While higher education is not the only culprit in institutionalized nonconsent, we recognize its power to replicate or challenge social and cultural norms and relations. Intellectual and emotional consent, we argue, are crucial components of radically inclusive higher education. Faculty members trained in feminist theory and anti-oppressive pedagogy who work to challenge power relations in their classrooms know this well. However, universities can serve as barriers to this work, for example, by discouraging the sharing of political opinions or personal information or by mandating that faculty report student disclosures of sexual assault and intimate partner violence (Cahill 2018). Ann Cahill (2018) argues that blanket mandatory reporting requirements do further violence to survivors:

> policies and practices about sexual harassment and violence . . . must remain aware—and even protective—of the vulnerability of vulnerability. . . . Legal or institutional encroachments upon [a survivor's] moment of disclosure, such as [mandatory reporting requirements], undermine its potential for intersubjective meaning-making while simultaneously rendering survivors even more vulnerable to invasive bureaucratic procedures that rarely result in justice. (6)

Blanket policies that violate or erase survivors' autonomy and agency are themselves violent and productive of more violence. We need policies, as Cahill suggests, that honor the vulnerability of disclosure and the importance of meaning-making and worldmaking. Misinterpretations and misapplications of Title IX requirements, along with the corporatization of higher education and the embrace of neoliberal norms and attitudes about students, teachers, and learning, prove to create a difficult environment for change. We have much to say about federal law and about neoliberalism and its implication in campuses of nonconsent in the upcoming chapters. But we argue that—even operating within the limitations of current structures—faculty, staff, students, and administration can and should work intentionally to find ways to shape courses, curricula, and campus policies with regard for student agency and boundaries.

## MAPPING CONSENT

In order to begin reconceptualizing consent, we turn first to feminist and antiracist theory and women of color feminisms, which have long been at the philosophical forefront of this work. Feminists were the first to argue in the 1970s and 1980s, for example, that women can and should consent and that sexual assault comprised all intimate activities that did not include mutual, clear, and ongoing consent—including within dating and marital relationships (Boston Women's Health Book Collective 1976; Brownmiller 1975; Firestone 1970; Millett 1970; Moraga 1983; Moraga and Anzaldúa 1981; Morgan 1970). Feminists, queer theorists, and antiracist theorists have also argued that sexual violence has a politics, and therefore that consent has a politics, too (Deer 2015; Hill Collins 2004; Moraga and Anzaldúa 1981; Winterich 2016). Consent is constrained by structural barriers (including abstinence-only education; sexist, racist, homophobic, and transphobic institutional policies and media portrayals; law enforcement and hospital staffs who are uneducated in how to interview survivors; and a legal system that often blames, shames, and retraumatizes survivors by, for example, requiring them to testify in court in the presence of the perpetrator). On the other hand, consent is enabled by empowering structures (including providing access to comprehensive and inclusive sex education; inclusive institutional policies and positive media portrayals; educated law enforcement and hospital staffs; and a legal system that does not blame, shame, or retraumatize survivors). In other words, consent cannot be separated from the social and cultural contexts within which it either thrives or weakens.

Moreover, just as feminist advocacy perspectives on violence acknowledge that assault and abuse extend beyond the physical to the emotional, intellectual, financial, and spiritual,[7] we expand current concepts of what consent can *mean* and *do* in higher education. Especially as higher education increasingly succumbs to neoliberal policies and practices that imagine students as consumers and education as a commodified service rather than a public good (Berg and Seeber 2016; Donoghue 2008; Nicolazzo 2015; Spencer and Patterson 2017; Wagner, Kulbaga, and Cohen 2017), it is imperative to think critically and in nuanced ways about consent and related concepts, such as agency, choice, free speech, and academic freedom. As such, this book critiques a neoliberal approach to imagining possibilities for consent and higher education. We are also interested in theorizing agency and dignity on campus—outside of neoliberal logics and especially for those most marginalized by hegemonic structures and attendant cultural narratives and myths (for example: "boys will be boys"; women and girls need protection; the myths of meritocracy, rugged individualism, and "overcoming" one's trauma or background; "It Gets Better"; and other instantiations of the White supremacist capitalist het-cis-patriarchy).[8]

We understand neoliberalism not merely as the defining logic of U.S. capitalism since 1980, but also as a *rationality* that (re)organizes everything—the law, the workplace, education, medicine, personal relationships, even human rights movements—in the economic terms of free-market fundamentalism (Brown 2015; Dingo 2012; Grewal 2005; Harvey 2007; Hesford 2011; Kulbaga 2008; Kulbaga 2016). In higher education, neoliberalism takes the form of so-called "responsibility-centered" management budget models, an increased focus on career services and teaching "career-ready" skills; a one-size-fits-all approach to online teaching that leaves teachers with little freedom to deviate from a factory-stamped course owned by the university; and a corporate model of governance that erodes or erases shared governance by administration and faculty and that perpetuates a rhetoric of budget crisis in order to justify top-down decision making, including about academics (Wagner, Kulbaga, and Cohen 2017). Neoliberal rationality envisions faculty, students, and other university actors as "good" or "bad" subjects according to their perceived, potential, or actual productivity and ability to bring in revenue. Within the context of the neoliberal university, consent education and policy emphasize individual students' behavior and decision making and reward "deserving" students who do not rock the boat, especially by identifying the violence of the institution and campus culture. As we explore throughout this book, neoliberalism cultivates and enables violence by individualizing and pathologizing it and by constructing victims and witnesses into categories of good and bad, pure and impure, blameless and blameworthy.

Discourses of freedom and choice that rely on a concept of neoliberal individuality threaten to erode and flatten the concepts of academic freedom and freedom of speech. Throughout this book, we argue that consent enables and cultivates—rather than threatens or curtails—free (academic) speech. In many contemporary public and academic conversations around such freedoms, however, all speech is constructed as equally valid, all rhetors as equally credible, and "ideological diversity" as under attack by "identity politics." In such a construction, free (academic) speech is equally available to all speakers and all students; no one has greater privilege as ideas freely circulate in the public square. Considering students' needs and boundaries when inviting speakers to campus, in this view, constrains the free speech of speakers. In reality, however, speakers—as well as students and faculty—have various levels of access to believability in public academic debate. A speaker such as Milo Yiannopoulos is able to wield his power and privilege against a transgender student precisely because Yiannopoulos and the student are not similarly situated to speak freely and safely. Our argument is that consent has implications for free speech and academic freedom and that cultivating it helps to open respectful conversations across myriad social and cultural locations of privilege and oppression. We recognize that the "marketplace of ideas" is not accessible to all. We aim to challenge such market rhetoric and hope to redistribute some of that agency.

On the topic of agency, Rebecca Stringer (2014) cautions against counterposing victimhood and agency. She argues that feminist discourse (including, in our experience, advocacy discourse) can repudiate the notion of women as victims (of violence, patriarchy, or other forms of oppression). The rejection of "victim" in favor of "survivor" denies the power of strategically claiming a victim identity as an agentic act. As Stringer puts it, and we concur, "suffering can be social, political and collective, rather than merely subjective, psychological and individual" (3). Furthermore, our anti-neoliberal approach to understanding consent resonates with Stringer's warning that the agent/victim dichotomy emerges from a worldview centered on personal responsibility that blames individuals for oppression (in general) and rape (in particular): "Exhorted to 'take responsibility,' the ideal neoliberal citizen is by definition self-blaming, their capacity for self-blame valued rather than problematized" (51). Some prefer the term "survivor"—a choice Stringer sees as an outgrowth of the idea that victimhood means self-blame (whereas "survivor" connotes taking responsibility). We reject the survivor/victim dichotomy as false, consistent with Stringer's argument about the agent/victim binary, and we believe that both terms can be valuable and meaningful in context. ("Victim," for example, has a legal meaning that "survivor" does not; "survivor" has an advocacy meaning that "victim" may not.) In other words, we affirm the right to self-identify, and we recognize the agency inherent in naming the forces of oppression that cause harm or make life unlivable. To name and resist oppression, individual and structural, including through victim discourse, requires and denotes strength and action, not weakness and passivity. Throughout this book, therefore, we use both *victim* and *survivor*, depending on which seems most appropriate for the context (see also, Freitag 2018; Harris 2011; Spry 1995).

We are also conscious of the structural barriers that make bearing witness to oppression difficult and that bring public judgment and censure to those who speak up and speak out. Women, people of color, queer, trans, and gender-nonconforming people are particularly at risk of being made subject to public discourses of doubt, blame, shame, and silencing that perpetuate discriminatory beliefs and attitudes and that favor the status quo. Leigh Gilmore (2017) argues that women and people of color are historically associated with lying (an association based partly in histories of being unable to testify in court, serve on juries, or vote). Furthermore, their narratives often run so against the grain of the normative American myth of self-reliance and self-making that they are "tasked with responsibilities they can never fully assume or discharge" (12)—as seen, for example, when women are held responsible for (not) being drugged, or when Black men are held responsible for (not) frightening White police officers. Victim blaming, along with other forms of judgment, attaches so regularly to sexual assault survivors who testify that it serves to deter many from reporting or testifying in the first place. In the context of sexual violence, for example, the "he said/she said" judgment creates a "realm of doubt that favors the rapist. . . . Consent, in this view, is a matter of interpretation" (Gilmore 2017, 6–7).

We are sympathetic to arguments that, like ours, acknowledge the limits of consent in a culture marked by institutionalized oppression and violence and interpersonal relationships often characterized by power differentials that limit mutual respect and agency. According to these critiques, affirmative consent policies and "Yes Means Yes" laws are well-meaning but naïve, at best rooted in an idealistic model of equality that does not (yet) exist and at worst unwittingly founded upon the inaccurate miscommunication model of consent, according to which better communication will eliminate the problem of violence (Harris 2018). In truth, sexual violence happens when someone feels entitled to disregard another's words, body language, actions, or other cues. Better communication does not solve the problem of entitlement and abuse of power. Some go further to reject the possibility of consent altogether, even in its most affirmative forms. Catherine MacKinnon (1983), for example, notoriously argues that heterosexuality is violent and unequal *by design*, writing that "If sex is normally something men do to women, the issue is less whether there was force and more whether consent is a meaningful concept" (650). More recently, using a queer and sex-positive approach, Joseph Fischel's (2019) *Screw Consent* suggests that consent is simply inadequate for capturing what he calls "pleasurable sexual justice politics," and other language is needed instead. While we agree with Fischel's suggestion that we proliferate the available language for pleasure and sexual justice, we are not ready to abandon the concept of consent altogether. First, while we frame consent as socially constructed and constrained, we reject MacKinnon's argument because it does not acknowledge the complexity of desire and agency around consent, such as exists in BDSM culture for example, and we want to make room for that complexity and agency. Second, consent has a legal, educational, and rhetorical history—a kind of thick context—that other terms may lack. In higher education contexts, which is our focus here, the word consent (even when poorly defined) is fairly ubiquitous in policy, campus communication, offices and programs, and education. As rhetorical and cultural critics, we are interested in both constructive critique of consent and productive reimagining of what the concept can mean and do.

Gilmore's (2017) caution that gender, race, and sexuality function to "produce sinking doubt and [to] legitimate violence" suggests the importance of reconceptualizing consent (and its opposite, violence) as socially and culturally constructed—and constructible (6). University campuses, we argue, are well situated to take up this crucial work. On campus, questions of agency and consent become salient, as students confront them in ways they may not have before. Colleges and universities function as *crucibles of consent* insofar as students may: (a) live on their own for the first time; (b) take classes that in both content and form differ markedly from what they experienced in high school, such that they must now engage with deep complexity, careful nuance, and thoughtful analysis with matters more serious and varied than the standard K-12 curriculum (especially given that school boards are wary of teaching politically "controversial" subjects such as gender-based violence); and (c) sometimes reside on campus, where pressure to be sexually active and even coercive can be persistent. Moreover, since universities are required by federal law to provide sexual assault awareness training and prevention, and since many high schools lack comprehensive and inclusive sex education, college campuses are places where students may discuss and define consent for the first time.

What, then, can cultivating consent mean on college campuses? We propose three interrelated types of consent (physical, emotional, and intellectual) in three contexts (individual, institutional, and pedagogical). Cultivating physical consent on campus means constructing a culture and set of policies that respects everyone's bodily autonomy and dignity, including their right to be free from violence, and their right to be believed and supported should they experience violence.[9] Physical safety and wellbeing are central to student learning. As we show above, however, violence disproportionately affects women, queer and trans students, and students of color. Institutional structures and supports can work to enable cultures of physical consent by providing inclusive, comprehensive health care, student services staff knowledgeable about mental health and trauma, and violence response staff (such as sexual assault advocates) knowledgeable in working with survivors of all backgrounds. Pedagogically, instructors can enable consent by acknowledging and addressing structural inequities and oppression, discussing violence with students openly and in an inclusive and survivor-centered way, and working to promote radical accessibility by being knowledgeable about mental health and trauma and by using trigger warnings to communicate respect for students' physical and emotional needs and "bodyminds" (Carter 2015).

Cultivating emotional consent on campus means working to establish trusting, respectful relationships among students and between students and faculty/staff. While administrators and instructors cannot (and ought not) dictate every relationship dynamic that exists on campus, campus culture can go a long way toward promoting knowledge of healthy relationships and establishing and respecting emotional boundaries within an inclusive framework that values all consensual relationships.[10] Moreover, hiring and promoting well-educated staff who are knowledgeable in common issues of emotional violence, trauma, and post-traumatic stress disorder will ensure that students with mental health needs are appropriately supported. Pedagogically, instructors can cultivate emotional consent by recognizing and respecting the reality of student mental health and wellbeing and by fostering classrooms responsive to that reality.

Cultivating intellectual consent on campus means constructing classrooms and campuses that value freedom of expression (including academic freedom) for teachers and learners. As we argue above, cultivating intellectual consent encourages such freedom of expression, rather than discouraging it, as some have suggested (Vatz 2016). This includes creating space for students to raise questions, to disagree, and to make mistakes without judgment, but with the expectation of improvement next time (Spencer 2015a). In communication, the concept of intellectual consent dovetails with invitational rhetoric, which critiques persuasion as a masculinist attempt to change someone else (Foss and Griffin 1995). At the institutional level, this means educating instructors, students, and staff about healthy intellectual debate and civic discourse, but without falling into the argument that all speech is equally acceptable or that all sides of an issue are equally valid. Respectful disagreement, without shaming or acting superior, is teachable (see Bone, Griffin, and Scholz 2008; Rood 2013, 2014; Spencer 2013; Spencer, Tyahur, and Jackson 2016). Intellectual consent is constrained by hate speech and other forms of conversational violence, including mansplaining (Solnit 2014), cissplaining, Whitesplaining, and other ways of disrespecting someone's conversational space.

Intellectual consent, as we see it, is an epistemological commitment to recognizing the validity of lived experience as a way of knowing, particularly for multiply minoritized people (see Allen 1996; Patterson 2018; Scott 2013). Gilmore (2017) argues that because women, people of color, and queer and trans people are often disbelieved when they speak out against oppressive actions or speech, including hate speech and verbal harassment—what she calls "objectivity's alignment against the oppressed" (13)—we need to conceive of bearing witness to their experiences differently. We argue that campuses must participate in the search for what she calls an "adequate witness . . . one who will receive testimony without deforming it by doubt, and without substituting different terms of value for the ones offered by the witness herself" (5). Pedagogically, cultivating intellectual consent means engaging in teaching practices that respect and acknowledge students' intellectual needs and boundaries while also reframing the terms of "objectivity" so that belief tilts toward, and not against, witnesses to injustice, even and especially if this means dethroning "objectivity" from its place of prominence in the discourse of higher education.

While our argument pertains to higher education generally, in the chapters that follow we sometimes take our campus as a case study to illustrate how broad national patterns play out in a particular context. This approach is consistent with our expertise as scholars working at the intersections of literary studies, cultural studies, and rhetorical criticism. We show that the examples we choose to focus on are neither extreme nor isolated. Ultimately, our expanded view of consent on campus aims to situate the conversation about sexual violence within a larger context that includes emotional and epistemic violence. If universities are serious about confronting the problem of sexual assault on campus, we must not isolate discussions of consent from other relevant conversations about power, oppression, agency, and violence, or hope that the Title IX office alone will adequately address it. In fact, we hold open the possibility in the following pages that institutional critique and cultural change is work that must be ongoing and constantly risks failure, since institutions are designed to excuse violence, and as Sara Ahmed (2016) suggests, the system is *not* broken when violence or harassment occur; instead it is precisely *working*. Our concept of consent nonetheless invites everyone on campus to challenge normative violence, to work toward meaningful change and the construction of campuses of consent.

## CHAPTER OVERVIEW

We have organized this book, roughly speaking, across a spectrum of consent, ranging from physical boundaries to emotional boundaries to intellectual boundaries. These categories often overlap, confirming the utility of our broadened conceptualization of consent. Chapter 1, "Just Response: Rethinking Communication and Consent in University Crime Alerts," considers the requirements of Title IX and the Clery Act, particularly the legal obligation of reporting crimes to the campus community and offering advice to students about how to prevent being victimized. Through an analysis of crime alerts on our campus as well as a critique of the Clery Act, we show how institutional language can blame survivors and perpetuate rape myths. Such language, we argue, does further violence to survivors as well as harming the campus by muddying the concepts of consent and violence. We then propose revised language, offering a way to comply with the imperfect law without advancing rape culture or engaging in institutional violence through language.

In chapter 2, "Stepping Up in a Safe Haven: Critiquing Campus Consent Initiatives," we analyze Haven, a for-profit program purchased by universities that provides students with an online training module about consent on campus, and Step UP!, a national corporate initiative aimed at encouraging bystander intervention. We argue that Haven and Step UP! traffic in neoliberal individualism, deflect community responsibility for consent, and ignore structural and systemic factors that produce inequity for women, queer, and trans students. We propose that instead of outsourcing the task of consent education to these one-size-fits-all online training initiatives, universities should draw on the resources of their own knowledgeable faculty and staff to provide ongoing, cross-disciplinary consent education throughout students' time on campus.

Chapter 3, "Consent Goes Viral: Searching for Positivity in Online Memes," turns to popular Internet memes as a meaningful, if dubitable, part of consent education. We argue that even largely praiseworthy and progressive messages about consent, such as the viral video "Consent: It's Simple As Tea," risk reifying harmful messages and gender stereotypes. We show how several popular memes define consent negatively, by what it is not, and we pose the question of what a positive understanding of consent might look like. Ultimately, we argue that while nonconsent is (about) violence, consent is about more than simply avoiding violence.

Chapter 4, "Trigger Warnings as Holistic Consent: A Social Justice Rationale," takes up the debate about trigger warnings in university classrooms. We suggest that many opponents of trigger warnings mischaracterize what trigger warnings are and what they do, as well as dismissing student mental health and perpetuating insidious myths about presumably endangered "free speech." We advise shifting the debate so that it is about making classrooms radically accessible to students with various trauma histories. Conceptualizing trigger warnings as a form of securing consent invites more and better participation of all students and faculty.

In chapter 5, "Survivor-Centered Pedagogy: Consentful Classrooms and Epistemic Justice," we continue to reflect on teaching theory and practice. Specifically, we consider how classrooms can become spaces in which violence—whether physical, emotional, or intellectual—is not dismissed but is instead meaningfully examined, theorized, and actively resisted. We call these *consentful classrooms*. We argue that a survivor-centered pedagogy is not solely about teaching content; it also works to decenter privileged ways of knowing and to foreground the epistemics and experiences of women, students of color, queer students, trans students, students with disabilities, and working-class students.

Finally, the conclusion, "Cultivating Campuses of Consent," offers some additional concrete suggestions for implementing our conception of radical consent in higher education. We offer recommendations about pedagogy, policy, and small, everyday behaviors—which we call *microaffections* and *microsubversions.* The arguments we make throughout the book are revisited and crystallized in concrete form in the conclusion. Ultimately, this book invites readers to join with us in the project of worldmaking—imagining and co-creating more just campuses and worlds.

---

## CHAPTER 1

# JUST RESPONSE

## RETHINKING COMMUNICATION AND CONSENT IN UNIVERSITY CRIME ALERTS

I n June 2016 Brock Turner became a household name when a California judge sentenced the Stanford student to a mere six months in prison for sexually assaulting an unconscious woman behind a dumpster. The judge's rationale that a longer sentence would have a harmful impact on Turner's future, as well as the lenient sentence itself, inspired a good deal of public controversy. Media coverage that emphasized Turner's now-thwarted potential Olympic swimming career and his parents' defense of his behavior cultivated discontent among activists, scholars, and student services professionals across the United States (Fantz 2016). Meanwhile, the woman he raped addressed him directly in court, saying:

> You don't know me, but you've been inside me, and that's why we're here today. . . . After a physical assault, I was assaulted with questions designed to attack me, to say see, her facts don't line up, she's out of her mind, she's practically an alcoholic, she probably wanted to hook up, he's like an athlete right, they were both drunk, whatever, the hospital stuff she remembers is after the fact, why take it into account, Brock has a lot at stake so he's having a really hard time right now. (Baker 2016)

In this case, the university, the sentencing judge, and Turner's family and friends identified sympathetically with Turner rather than the woman he attacked—an example of what philosopher of misogyny Kate Manne (2018) calls *himpathy*, the "excessive sympathy sometimes shown to male perpetrators of sexual violence" in the attempt to preserve their reputation, power, or status (197). In a written statement to the judge, Turner's father, Dan Turner, minimized the assault, calling it "20 minutes of action" that should not have such a severe impact on his son's future. As feminists have long argued, this kind of response exemplifies a fundamental tenet of rape culture, which minimizes sexual assault and blames victims for a range of behaviors and choices that presumably led to ambiguity about consent. While we do not equate justice with a longer prison term, we do regard the Turner case as representative of the persistence of rape culture and the continued need for discussion about consent and appropriate responses to sexual violence.[1]

Notably, Turner's case inspired outrage as well as himpathy, and invited and renewed conversations about rape culture and consent on campus. Against the backdrop of the Turner case, we began the fall 2016 semester at our public university with a campus-wide notification of a sexual assault in a fraternity house on the weekend before the first day of class, followed by another similar alert a few weeks afterward. As required by federal law, most notably the Clery Act,[2] our university's "Crime Alerts" explained the basic facts of both incidents, then concluded by encouraging students to obtain consent and by offering tips to prevent sexual assault. The language of these crime alerts, however, was disturbing for a number of reasons: consent was not clearly defined; the role of drinking (specifically illegal, underage drinking) was overemphasized, leading to victim blaming; and finally, the prevention tips placed the onus on potential targets of assault (for instance, to be aware of their surroundings) instead of potential perpetrators (for instance, to obtain clear and enthusiastic consent). When we mentioned our concerns to the staff members whose office posts these bulletins, they replied that the language is required by federal law as well as by the definitions of rape and sexual assault in the Ohio criminal code.

But the precise language used in our university's crime alerts is *not* required by federal law. In this chapter, we set out to accomplish three goals: first, we provide a history and feminist analysis of the Clery Act, the problematically paternalistic and consumer-focused federal law that requires universities to provide timely crime notifications to the campus community. Next, we offer a critique of the language of our university's publicly communicated responses to sexual assault (the Crime Alerts). Finally, we advocate for a more feminist, accurate, and effective way of notifying campus communities about sexual assault while complying with imperfect federal law. We argue that all campus communication about sexual violence, including the crime alerts and reports required by the Clery Act, should be survivor-centered and should aim to cultivate safety, accountability, prevention, and healing for individual survivors as well as for the campus community.

As we analyze our university's crime alerts, we recognize the impossibility of treating "the university" as a coherent and monolithic entity. The details of a university's overall response to any given case will include interactions with myriad campus offices and with potentially supportive and feminist-informed students, staff, and faculty. But however sensitive and effective the university's response may or may not be in individual instances (note here our university's previous failure to comply with Clery, which resulted in a sanction in 2005), we focus as rhetorical critics on the official communication that gets circulated to tens of thousands of people several times a year, whenever sexual violence is reported. Even if the staff responsible for working with students who have experienced assault do their jobs perfectly, the university crime alerts dangerously mystify sexual violence as well as consent.

## CLARIFYING THE CLERY ACT: PROTECTING WHOM?

The Clery Act—passed originally in 1990 and expanded several times since, most recently in 2013 as an update to the Violence Against Women Act (VAWA)—is a "consumer protection law" (Clery Center 2017) that aims to hold universities accountable for transparency in crime reporting, policy, and prevention. Originally, the law required institutions receiving federal funding to write and distribute annual crime reports; later amendments stipulated that they provide "timely warnings and emergency notifications" of crimes covered by the act to all students, faculty, and staff. The VAWA amendments broaden these requirements to focus on victims' rights as well as sexual assault education and programming.

While we understand that universities must comply with the Clery Act, we also contend that its letter and spirit are fundamentally conservative and patriarchal, based on the assumption that mandated crime reporting, emergency alerts, and awareness of security protocol will effectively "protect" vulnerable students—especially young White women—from harm. We believe that encouraging students to be aware of crime, and to report crime, in hopes of protecting themselves from sexual violence is at odds with more progressive and feminist approaches to campus sexual assault adjudication and policy that center the experiences and needs of survivors. Historically, the Clery Act can be situated in a larger conservative political backlash against progressive rape law reform. Michelle J. Anderson (2016) argues that "in the 1990s, as a result of a series of high-profile cases involving the rape and murder of children by strangers, the conservative, tough-on-crime movement that had focused on the drug war began to shift its focus to sex offenders" (1954). This shift resulted in a harmful focus on mandatory minimum sentences, shaming sanctions such as Megan's Laws, and statutes that construct sexual violence as exceptional rather than routine, characterized by injurious physical force, and therefore in need of stiff prison sentences (1955–1956).[3] She notes that "these changes were conservative and punitive. They were fueled not by the feminist movement, but by politicians reacting to notorious and rare cases of child abduction, rape, and murder" (1954). Resistance to progressive reform *on campus* shares some similarities, though not the zeal for draconian punishments for accused students. Rather, it humanizes college students accused of sexual assault, constructs them "himpathetically" (Manne 2018) as in need of special protection against broadened feminist definitions of rape in order to guard their valuable "bright futures" (Anderson 1992). Meanwhile, students who report sexual assault are dehumanized, cast as unreliable, inexperienced, vindictive, or confused by Title IX, feminist definitions of rape, and mandatory university consent trainings. Anderson explains:

The story of manipulative feminists making victims out of otherwise well-adjusted undergraduates fits into a broader popular narrative that campuses have become bastions of "sexual paranoia," filled with trigger-warning-happy activists trying to herd coeds from psychological harm. It coincides with the position that this generation of students is coddled and unprepared for the real world, and that the safe spaces they seek are "infantilizing and anti-intellectual" and "may be teaching students to think pathologically." (1992)[4]

On the one hand, the conservative backlash suggests, feminism has created "sexual paranoia" on campus through progressive sexual assault education and policy; on the other, feminism is not concerned *enough* with the "real" problems: that young women in college are drinking, engaging in sexting and hookups, and learning about affirmative consent and the right to sexual autonomy. On the one hand, conservatives are concerned about accused students' rights, humanity, and bright futures (rather than victims'); on the other, they focus on victims' sexual "purity" or lack thereof, and obscure the responsibility of perpetrators whose sexual history is not put on trial (Gilmore 2017; Solnit 2016). Given this regressive context, feminist scholars must question the Clery Act's original intent as well as its ultimate effects.

In addition to questioning the backlash context of Clery, we must ask if the personal responsibility model implicit in crime reporting requirements is part of a larger ideology of neoliberalism that affects all aspects of higher education, including sexual assault policy and rhetoric (Spencer and Patterson 2017; Wagner, Kulbaga, and Cohen 2017). The language of the reporting requirement of the law inaccurately constructs crime alerts as capable of mitigating threats and preventing future crimes:

Each institution . . . shall make timely reports to the campus community on crimes considered to be a threat to other students and employees . . . that are reported to campus security or local law police agencies. Such reports shall be provided to students and employees in a manner that is timely, that withholds the names of victims as confidential, . . . and that will aid in the prevention of similar occurrences. (Clery Act f [3])

We contend that in practice, the reporting components of the Clery Act, as interpreted by many institutions of higher education, contribute to the proliferation of what Gotell (2008) calls "discourses of responsibilization and risk management" (866) that construct normative sexual subjects in a neoliberal campus economy. Clery envisions young women who are either "good girls" (including ideal victims who practice appropriate caution even if they "fail") or "at risk" (including queer and low-income students and students of color); however, the act envisions young men who are "good" when they secure consent and avoid criminalization. This specific expression of neoliberal governmentality "prescribe[s] privileged sexual subjectivities and new conceptions of good/credible victims [as well as] new mechanisms for discrediting claims of sexual assault" (Gotell 2008, 866). By assuming that an informed student (consumer) will be a protected student (consumer), campuses—complying with the Clery Act—reify personal student responsibility and risk management at the expense of more survivor-centered and collective approaches to campus sexual violence.

The history of the Clery Act is instructive in this regard. The Jeanne Clery Disclosure of Campus Security Policy and Campus Crime Statistics Act was passed in 1990, after the rape and murder of a nineteen-year-old White student at Lehigh University in 1986. Twenty-year-old Josoph M. Henry, a Black student at Lehigh, was promptly arrested and later convicted of the crime. But Jeanne Ann Clery's parents were dismayed to learn of other recent violent crimes at Lehigh. They sued the school for negligence and began advocating for federally mandated campus reporting of all crime in an effort to inform and protect students and to advise parents of the safety of specific campuses. In interviews, the Clerys described believing they were making a "safe choice" when they sent their daughter to Lehigh, and they would not have permitted her to attend if they had known about the comparatively high levels of crime there (Gross and Fine 1990). The Clerys' advocacy on behalf of mandated federal crime reporting, which eventually resulted in the Clery Act, must be contextualized in a wider discourse about sexual violence that characterizes late-twentieth-century public culture: a masculinist rhetoric of protection and a corresponding rhetoric of "crisis" or "panic" that is bound up with widespread anxiety about young women's and girls' sexuality and vulnerability (Anderson 2016; Gilmore 2017; Oliver 2015). This rhetoric prioritizes the protection of young, White women attending college, like Jeanne Clery, who are assumed to be "innocent" and "pure" and therefore particularly in need of such protection (Berlant 1997; Deer 2015; Grewal 2005; Gotell 2008; Solnit 2016), and it has resulted in legislative priorities focused on "consumer protection" and other neoliberal goals (Anderson 2016). Because Jeanne Clery was White and her assailant Black, there are racialized aspects to the Clery Act's reporting requirements as well, especially given the disproportionate profiling, criminalization, and imprisonment of Black men in the United States in the latter half of the twentieth century, as well as the longer history of racialized and gendered discourse that justified lynching by portraying Black men as ever-present sexual threats to "pure," unwilling White women (Alexander 2012; Hill Collins 2004).

Thus, while the 2013 VAWA amendments to the Clery Act expand its work in important ways beyond crime reporting and emergency alerts, the original legislation arose out of a (gendered and racialized) concern that students and parents were not being adequately notified of criminal dangers, as well as a corresponding assumption that knowledge of crime would reduce risk and provide protection for vulnerable young women. Originally, the law did just that: mandated that universities collect and disseminate crime statistics regularly. Griffin and colleagues (2017) note that Clery "was originally designed as 'consumer friendly' legislation" (403) that would enable students and parents to factor campus safety into their college decisions. Ironically, the VAWA amendments to the Clery Act, which were intended to address the limitations of the law's original emphasis on crime reporting, do not always inform the language of crime alerts and reports—perhaps because crime alerts and reports are often the responsibility of campus law enforcement or public relations personnel, who may or may not receive training from the Title IX office, women's centers, or community antiviolence advocates. As we show in the next section, emergency crime alerts are a particularly problematic aspect of Clery Act compliance, especially when they are not handled in ways that are inclusive, survivor-centered, and informed by feminist work in sexual assault advocacy and prevention.

This work has been central in conceptualizing consent in feminist terms, and in framing violence as primarily a *social* justice, not a *criminal* justice, issue. Julie Novkov (2016) provocatively suggests that using laws such as Clery as the primary lens through which to shape policy misses the point that we can gain much from "thinking about assault accusations as community wrongs rather than individual wrongs" so that campuses can focus "on structures rather than on individual-level analysis of consent and intent" (592; see also Deer 2015). In other words, feminist and antiviolence educators and advocates understand gendered violence as an issue of power and oppression, a key tool in patriarchal control of women and other disempowered groups. Framing rape as a community wrong honors this perspective and, importantly, works to construct a less oppressive community. The alternative, dealing with accusations of sexual assault as the behavioral problems of individuals, often means that campuses treat criminal felonies not as crimes, but as violations of university codes of honor. As Oliver (2015) explains, universities have a vested interest not so much in reducing the actual harm of sexual assault as they do in mitigating public perception that students on their campuses are vulnerable to sexual assault. Universities accomplish this by minimizing sexual assault, either by inserting diminutive adjectives in front of the word "rape" (e.g., party rape, date rape, acquaintance rape) or by referring to sexual assault as *nonconsensual sex*. Oliver (and those trained in feminist antiviolence advocacy) understands *nonconsensual sex* as a logical impossibility; the term serves as a euphemism for rape, not another class of behavior, and certainly not a form of sex. As Sarah Deer (2015) insists, "there is no such thing as nonviolent rape" (xix), and rape myths—including "the 'nice guy' who accidentally has nonconsensual sex" (xix)—function to normalize and excuse violence. Leigh Gilmore (2017) further argues that, in cases of sexual violence, objectivity "align[s] against the oppressed" (13), so much so that consent becomes "a matter of interpretation" (6–7) and students who report rape on campus are "tainted" witnesses (2), presumed to be unreliable. In Novkov's (2016) language, legal frameworks "presen[t] a countervailing set of incentives to establish investigative and disciplinary systems that will limit [universities'] exposure to legal challenges" (603)—and, we might add, limit survivors' willingness to seek support.

In any case, there is convincing evidence that the crime reporting requirements of the Clery Act are largely ineffective (Janosik and Gehring, 2003; Janosik and Plummer, 2005; Kiss and White, 2016; Richards et al., 2017). Most students and parents do not read the mandated crime reports, and those who do read them do not factor them into college choices (Janosik and Gehring, 2003; Janosik and Plummer, 2005). Most students say that they "feel safe" on campus regardless of crime reports (Janosik and Gehring, 2003). Kiss and White (2016) suggest that one barrier is that administrators may worry that increased education and Clery Act compliance may lead to higher levels of reporting, reflecting poorly on the university's reputation (102). On the other hand, 77 percent of university presidents believe that sexual violence is not a problem on their campuses, reflecting a bias in favor of minimizing or denying prevalent crime (Richards et al. 2017, 112). Guffey (2013) found that Clery Act data from universities was often at odds with data from survivor services organizations, showing that the data collected by universities is incomplete at best and inaccurate at worst. Finally, Gardner (2015) argues that the Clery Act is unclear, expensive to implement, and burdensome for college administrators, and that its impact on campus safety is minimal.

Even feminist scholars who believe the Clery Act has had a positive impact argue that universities often do the technical minimum to comply with the law, rather than committing to what Kiss and White (2016, passim) call "an ethic of caring" on campus. And according to Tara N. Richards et al. (2017), in campus responses to sexual assault cases, "the focus often remains on official reporting and bureaucratic structures, rather than addressing and healing the whole person" (112). Beyond the crime reporting requirements, other feminist scholars have pointed out that few universities are in full compliance of the expanded Clery Act requirements for education, prevention, and bystander intervention programming. For example, Griffin et al. (2017) found that only 11 percent of schools within their sample were fully compliant with the Campus Sexual Violence Elimination Act of 2013 (SaVE Act), the section of VAWA that expanded Clery to include a range of required sexual assault programming, prevention, and education (401). On average, each school met only slightly more than half of the criteria (10 out of 18) for compliance with the SaVE Act, while 30.1 percent of schools had low compliance, and only 11.2 percent had high compliance (412). Noncompliance was most often seen in regard to providing clear and easy-to-access information about sexual assault programs, bystander intervention, and interpersonal violence. Higher compliance was seen in regard to providing definitions and statistics about sexual violence (412). In other words, universities eager to comply with Clery often prioritize providing information (crime alerts, definitions, statistics) over more proactive and expensive—but arguably more effective—educational efforts.

However, education is not necessarily the same as prevention. Ultimately, it may be that sexual violence is *not* preventable, at least not without radical anti-oppressive social and cultural change. In that case, a focus on crime reporting is dubious at best, since most sexual assault survivors choose not to report. Universities could focus less on presumably "protective" crime reporting and prevention—since these in fact protect universities from lawsuits or negative press, and do not protect students from violence—and more on fostering supportive environments for victims and survivors. We realize that this may be an unpopular argument because it does not allow legislators, parents, or universities to feel in control of sexual assault incidence, prevalence, or reporting. But it *is* a more supportive argument for survivors of violence, who benefit from language and policies that validate the reality of their experiences and that do not contribute to a culture that minimizes or denies its existence or effects, or that blames victims for presumably poor choices. In this connection, the assumption that prevention is possible harms victims by suggesting that they could have prevented the crime. Consider, for comparison's sake, the model of suicide prevention, which also affects college campuses. Effective suicide prevention programming acknowledges, despite its name, that prevention is *not* always possible. It works to reduce suicide incidence when possible, but it also supports survivors of suicide attempts as well as friends and loved ones (Mental Health Association of Maryland, Missouri Department of Mental Health, and National Council for Behavioral Health 2013).

Protectionist approaches to sexual assault on college campuses may be well meaning, but they go against the best practices of feminist advocacy and support services for victims and survivors. They also individualize the problem as a neoliberal matter of consumer protection, rather than addressing the contexts of power and oppression that make sexual assault prevalence so high on college campuses. Despite these critiques of the Clery Act, we believe that universities can comply with the crime reporting and emergency alerts requirements in ways that acknowledge the reality of sexual violence and that affirm survivors' needs (to be believed, validated, supported, and able to choose how best to proceed). In the next section, we provide a feminist critique of the language in our university's fall 2016 crime alerts. We then offer an alternative version that improves on the shortcomings of our university's language.

## NAMING, SHAMING, AND BLAMING

As we have said, colleges and universities must conform to the requirements of federal law, which currently include reporting crime to the campus community and sharing crime prevention tips. But campus crime notices can certainly go *beyond* the minimum requirements of these laws, and they can respond to these laws with a feminist, just, and advocacy-based approach. Indeed, a university ought to empower and educate students, as well as to support and heal survivors, ultimately constructing a more just world. Unfortunately, many universities' reporting practices work against this goal.

Ours included. On Thursday, August 25, 2016, just before the start of fall semester at the large public university in Ohio where we work, a student reported to noncampus police that a man she knew raped her in a fraternity house located near campus. As required by the Clery Act, our university posted a "Crime Alert" to the internal campus website, followed by a list of "Crime Reduction Tips" and other information about sexual assault. The tips included boilerplate "if you see something, say something" advice, as well as recommendations to "practice legal low-risk drinking" and "if you feel uncomfortable with friends or strangers remove yourself from the situation and seek help"

## CRIME ALERT: SEXUAL ASSAULT REPORTED OFF CAMPUS

**All [University]**

A female student reported to the [City] Police Department that she was sexually assaulted by a male known to her at an unidentified fraternity house in the city of _____. This incident is reported to have occurred in the early morning hours on Thursday, August 25, 2016.

No additional information is available at this time. [City] Police are investigating the report.

**Crime Reduction Tips:**
1. If you see something, say something.
2. Consent is required for all sexual activity; persons who are intoxicated may not be capable of consent.
3. Please practice legal low-risk drinking.
4. If you feel uncomfortable with friends or strangers remove yourself from the situation and seek help.

**REMEMBER:** Alcohol and other drugs lower inhibitions, increasing perpetration and decreasing defenses.

**UPD** reminds the community of the Sexual Assault Prevention and Response Program located at _____ Health Services Center, available to victims of sex-based offenses, including sexual violence, sexual misconduct, domestic/dating violence, and stalking.

*Figure 1. Crime Alert from August 25, 2016.*

(fig. 1). The admonition against drinking recurs below the list of tips: "Alcohol and other drugs lower inhibitions, increasing perpetration and decreasing of defenses." Finally, information about our university's advocacy and support services through the Sexual Assault Prevention and Response Program appears at the very bottom of the alert.

The federal requirement that universities promptly report all incidents of sexual assault (along with other crimes) also requires language about crime prevention and campus education programs related to crime—in an effort, according to the language of the Clery Act— "to encourage students and employees to be responsible for their own security and the security of others." Clery assumes that dissemination of information about crimes and crime prevention will have an adverse effect on crime, which is a dubious assumption and a potentially victim-blaming one, given its focus on individual vigilance and "good" choices. However, universities may conform to these legal requirements in ways that do not attach blame to survivors (or potential targets in advance). In our university's effort to follow the law, we identify several problems: first, the "Crime Reduction Tips" focus almost exclusively on targets' behavior, contributing to rape culture by perpetuating victim-blaming mentalities about sexual assault. Indeed, following a crime report with a list of prevention tips itself implies assumptions about the presumably wrong choices made by the victim of the crime just described (for example, she should have removed herself from the situation, and/or she should not have been drinking). Second, the tips themselves seem largely uninformed by feminist theory and advocacy about sexual assault. For example, nothing about "legal" drinking reduces crime (with the exception of the crime of underage drinking). Moreover, besides focusing solely on targets' behavior and responsibility for preventing crime, "practice legal low-risk drinking" and "if you feel uncomfortable . . . remove yourself from the situation" are not necessarily practical or effective ways of avoiding assault. For example, if the victim knows the perpetrator, as 80 percent do (U.S. Department of Justice 2000) and as the victim in this case did, then she may feel supremely comfortable with him. Further, if the perpetrator drugs his victim's first drink, then "low-risk drinking" is beside the point. (In any case, even "high-risk" drinking does not invite or excuse violent behavior.) Finally, but crucially, these tips imply that sexual assault results from lowered inhibitions and decreased defenses. Sexual assault is a crime of power, privilege, and entitlement, not misunderstanding or fumbling or losing control, and it is used systematically and knowingly (including on college campuses) to oppress women, queer and trans people, and others who lack power within a patriarchal institution. Failing to acknowledge this depoliticizes gendered violence.[5]

Remarkably, in our university's "Crime Reduction Tips," alcohol consumption appears three times: first in tip number 2, "Consent is required for all sexual activity; persons who are intoxicated may not be able to consent"; second in tip 3, described above, "Please practice legal low-risk drinking"; and third in the all-caps "REMINDER" that "alcohol and other drugs lower inhibitions, increasing perpetration and decreasing defenses." While we do not entirely oppose educating the campus community about excessive alcohol consumption, this level of repetition seems to suggest that, if college students simply never drank alcohol, they would be safe from harm. Not only is that false, it is also blaming. Students who drink when they are assaulted—especially if they are underage—already often avoid reporting the crime because of shame or embarrassment about that behavior, or fear that they will be disciplined by the university or law enforcement (Shaw 2016). This shame is compounded, of course, by the humiliation and guilt that are consequences of sexual assault in the first place. A university that wishes to empower and educate students about consent and sexual assault (as well as to support and heal survivors) should work to avoid even the slightest appearance of blaming victims for lowered inhibitions or "decreas[ed] defenses." Relatedly, the excessive focus on alcohol consumption largely erases the perpetrator from its judgment, echoing Solnit's (2016) point that patriarchy absolves perpetrators of agency or blame, while attaching blame and shame to victims. While potential perpetrators *are* the focus of the phrases "consent is required" and "increasing perpetration," the bulk of the recommendation to avoid alcohol is clearly directed at survivors and potential targets.[6] In fact, the language of the "Crime Reduction Tips" at our university, as shown in this example, seems implicitly to construct students who choose to drink as making "irresponsible" choices that lead to potential assaults. If the Clery Act aims (in its own words) "to encourage students and employees to be responsible for their own security and the security of others," then the "irresponsible" students presumably put their security and others' at risk and become victims. Note that the *target's* irresponsibility, and *not* the perpetrator's, gets named (and blamed) here. This construction requires individual students (disproportionately women, trans, and queer)[7] to bear the burden of their own safety, security, and right to be free from violence—rather than a construction in which the university community works proactively to foster nonviolent spaces, deconstruct rape culture, and support survivors.

Just over two weeks after we received the first alert, on September 14, 2016, our university issued a second Crime Alert, this one describing two incidents of sexual assault (fig. 2). In both cases, the perpetrators knew their victims. In the second incident, the description focuses on the victim's behavior leading up to the assault: "A female student told . . . police that Saturday, September 10, she and a male acquaintance were dancing at a bar . . . when the male inappropriately touched her and refused to stop." Immediately below the descriptions of the two incidents is the statement "[Our] University and [city] police advise students to be aware of their surroundings and to be with friends." We find it curious that, although both incidents involved perpetrators acquainted with their victims, the language of the crime alert maintains that being "with friends" will ensure (or at least increase) safety and reduce crime. In fact, as already noted, acquaintances, friends, and dates make up a vast majority of perpetrators of sexual assault specifically and gendered violence more generally. The juxtaposition, in this alert, between the descriptions of the incidents and the advice to be with friends (she was dancing with a friend!) highlights the misconstrual of agency we mentioned above and points to the urgent need for a basic understanding in the alert of how sexual assault works and who deserves blame for it. Moreover, focusing on the second victim's choice to be out dancing with the perpetrator is unnecessary to the alert (and is certainly not required by the Clery Act). Why, then, does the alert describe her actions at all? Whatever the reason, the practical effect of the description suggests, quite clearly, that her actions were likely to blame, or were at least questionable. This is the exact opposite of education and empowerment; it in fact teaches students and the campus community that perpetrators are not at fault, that friends are safe even when they are precisely not, and that dancing is not

# INFORMATION BULLETIN: SEXUAL ASSAULTS REPORTED OFF CAMPUS

All [University]
[City] police report two sexual assaults in recent days.

1. Police say a female reported a sexual assault by a male acquaintance in the early morning hours of Sept. 9. The incident was reported in an outdoor area in the _____ block of _____ Street.

   The suspect was identified as a [University] student, but no description was provided.

2. A female student told [City] police that Saturday, Sept. 10, she and a male acquaintance were dancing at a bar in the _____ block of _____ when the male inappropriately touched her and refused to stop.

   The student identified the male and police are investigating.

   [University] and [City] police advise students to be aware of their surroundings and be with friends. Part of "I am _____" includes watching out for each other.

**Crime Reduction Tips:**
1. If you see something, say something. Part of "I am _____" includes watching out for each other.
2. Consent is required for all sexual activity; persons who are intoxicated may not be capable of consent.
3. Alcohol is involved in most campus crimes; if you choose to drink, please practice legal low-risk drinking.
4. Trust your instincts; if you feel uncomfortable with friends or strangers remove yourself from the situation.

**REMEMBER:** Alcohol and other drugs lower inhibitions, increasing perpetration and decreasing defenses.

We remind the community of the Sexual Assault Prevention and Response Program located at _____ Health Services Center, available to victims of sex-based offenses, including sexual violence, sexual misconduct, domestic/dating violence, and stalking. [University's] Campus Safety and Security website has information and resources about sexual assault and other interpersonal crimes.

*Figure 2. Crime Alert from September 14, 2016.*

appropriately being aware of one's surroundings. Furthermore, reading such a crime alert—far from reducing crime or making students safer—risks triggering survivors of sexual assault, including the very students who reported the crimes in the first place.

The university staff charged with conforming to the Clery Act most likely do not wish to do harm or blame victims.[8] Instead, the specific language of our institution's response to the law is a way to try to avoid negative press or legal attention while seeming to do something about violence. While these may be relevant concerns for administrators, they should *not* be the main concern of university crime alerts in response to sexual assault, even when conforming to law. That language exacerbates survivors' already acute anxieties about facing incredulity or blame or having their experiences rationalized or minimized. Instead, crime alerts should take lessons from advocacy contexts and make the survivor's needs central. This includes, at a minimum, the need for validation, safety, accountability, healing, and cultural change.

While each survivor has a unique experience, the humiliating personal and spiritual[9] violation that characterizes sexual assault, coupled with the ubiquity of victim blaming and minimizing, means that survivors will often confront shame, guilt, and self-doubt, which need attention from trained advocates. Given that a survivor's healing is often directly affected by the response she receives when she first reports the incident (Krivoshey et al. 2013), universities have a moral obligation to cultivate compassionate, knowledgeable responses, including in the crime alerts sent to every student, faculty, and staff member. Well-meaning administrators, faculty, and staff may *want* to help, but without training in sexual assault advocacy, they may do more harm than good. For example, encouraging survivors to press criminal charges can wrest control of the situation from them or threaten their autonomy and agency. Institutional news bulletins should not replicate the loss of control a survivor experienced during an assault.

In much of the literature on campus sexual assault, scholars confound the issue by using language about "gray areas" or "ambiguity" about what sexual assault is and what consent means (see Shaw 2016). Universities that do not provide clear definitions of consent in their crime alerts—either because staff responsible for conforming to law and policies are not adequately trained in sexual assault law and advocacy, or because they fall in line with cultural myths about what violence is, who may be victims, and who gives and receives consent—also contribute to mystifying the issue. Very often, these myths align with cultural constructions of gender, gender identity, and sexuality, leading to misperceptions that contribute to rape culture. For example, cultural norms construct cisgender men as sexual aggressors (subjects and agents) and (usually cisgender) women as passive objects to be pursued. We reject definitions of consent that rely on stereotypes in which everyone identifies as heterosexual and cisgender, men always pursue, and women have the sole responsibility of "unambiguous" consent. While statistically speaking, men constitute a full 90 percent of perpetrators of sexual violence and 90 percent of sexual violence victims are women, this does not mean that men do not experience violence or that women are always passive and lack sexual agency. Indeed, such gender stereotypes play a central role in rape culture by erasing both women's agency and men's responsibility. Men are more likely to commit sexual violence in communities where sexual violence goes unpunished and where narrow conceptions of masculinity are normalized (Fahlberg and Pepper 2016; Kilmartin and Berkowitz 2005; Rozee and Koss 2001). Not only do they exacerbate violence, but these stereotypes also exclude and potentially alienate students who do not conform to narrow cultural scripts of gender and sexuality, including trans and gender-nonconforming students. Accurate and effective definitions of consent need more useful and current understandings of masculinity, femininity, sexuality, and agency.

Moreover, campus alerts can also buttress rape culture when they suggest that alcohol consumption, age, being with strangers, or going dancing makes consent complicated or ambiguous. This invites the question, what counts as sexual assault? Whose violation counts as legitimate? The power—of scholars, university staff, law enforcement, or laws themselves—to wield language about sexual violence is a productive form of power, and it shapes who is seen as agents, whose agency is erased or obscured, and whose futures get figured as valuable and important. We maintain that, from both a legal standpoint (at least according to Ohio law) and an advocacy standpoint, consent is relatively clear. It is rape *culture* that depends on ideas of ambiguity around consent (see Valenti 2014). This is the case despite the fact that Ohio law only indirectly defines consent. For example, according to the Ohio Alliance to End Sexual Violence (OAESV)'s "Fact Sheet of Legal Definitions" (2012), rape includes the following situations:

- Offender has sexual conduct with another AND
- The offender substantially impaired the other in order to prevent resistance (through drugs, intoxicant, or controlled substance) by force, threat of force, or deception); OR
- The other person is younger than 13 years old.; OR
- The other person's ability to resist or consent is impaired due to mental or physical condition or advanced age, and the offender knows this OR
- Sexual conduct where the offender uses force or threat of force. (OAESV 2012)

The law clearly outlines rape as sexual conduct with lack of consent, whether through intoxication, age, disability, or force or threat. This law offers a negative definition of consent (what it is not) rather than a positive one (what it is),[10] but legally speaking, there exists little "gray area" to mull over here. Nonetheless, our university, in its email response to our stated concerns about the crime alerts, highlighted the ambiguity of the phrase "substantially impaired" in order to explain the thrice-repeated admonishment against drinking therein.

Despite the problems we have identified in this chapter with the Clery Act and with campus crime alerts, we support the new provisions in the 2013 VAWA, which require universities to hire trained sexual assault advocates to serve and support student survivors and to create programming that fosters a clearer understanding of consent and violence in the campus community.[11] At the time of this writing, however, Secretary of Education Betsy DeVos is trying to roll back some of these measures in an effort to "protect" the accused on campus. Nonetheless, we contend that while laws like Clery provide a minimum standard to which universities must conform, colleges and universities ought to go beyond the minimum, and beyond the law, to foster a campus that is educated, survivor-centered, supportive, just, and livable for all students. Such work can begin (but should not end) with the language used by the university in its communication, including in campus crime notices.

In the table below (fig. 3), we provide suggestions for better language in our university's crime alerts, informed by feminist advocacy principles. In writing these revised tips, we observed the following guidelines, which we commend to the attention of readers who share our commitments to better reporting language:

- The description of the crime should not focus on the survivor's actions or behavior before the assault.
- The description of the crime should use active voice and syntax that puts the perpetrator in the subject position in the sentence (e.g., not "she was reportedly attacked" but "a known assailant reportedly attacked her").
- The crime prevention tips should not be targeted solely at potential victims but at the entire campus community.
- The crime prevention tips should not construct a hierarchy of a potential victims' "good/responsible" or "bad/irresponsible" choices.
- In general, the crime prevention tips should not focus on targets' behavior or choices in any way, but instead on defining sexual assault according to state law and consent according to feminist principles.
- While acknowledging that our state law does define *rape* as sex with someone who is incapacitated by alcohol or drugs, the crime prevention tips should not put the onus on targets' choice to avoid alcohol consumption, nor should it construe "legal" drinking as less likely to result in crime.

If we compare the language of the Clery Act, which requires crime reporting and crime prevention tips, with the language of our university's crime alerts, and then with our suggested language, the differences are striking (see fig. 3).

## CLERY ACT
f (3)
Each institution participating in any program under this subchapter and part C of subchapter I of chapter 34 of title 42, other than a foreign institution of higher education, shall make timely reports to the campus community on crimes considered to be a

## OUR UNIVERSITY'S CRIME ALERTS

**Crime Alert 1**
A female student reported to the [City] Police Department that she was sexually assaulted by a male known to her at an unidentified fraternity house in the city of _____. This incident is reported to have occurred in the early morning hours on Thursday, August 25, 2016.

**Crime Alert 2**
[City] Police report two sexual assaults in recent days.
1.  Police say a female reported a sexual assault by a male acquaintance in the early morning hours of Sept. 9. The incident was reported in an outdoor area *[sic] in the _____ block of _____ Street.*

The suspect was identified as a [University] student, but no description was provided.

2.  A female student told [City] police that Saturday, Sept. 10, she and a male acquaintance were dancing at a bar in the _____ block of _____ when the male inappropriately touched her and refused to stop.

The student identified the male and police are investigating.

**Crime Alert 1**
Crime Reduction Tips:
1.  If you see something, say something.
2.  Consent is required for all sexual activity; persons who are intoxicated may not be capable of consent.
3.  Please practice legal low-risk drinking.
4.  If you feel uncomfortable with friends or strangers, remove yourself from the situation and seek help.

**REMEMBER:** Alcohol and other drugs lower inhibitions, increasing perpetration and decreasing defenses.

**Crime Alert 2**
Crime Reduction Tips:
1.  If you see something, say something. Part of "I Am _____" includes watching out for each other.
2.  Consent is required for all sexual activity; persons who are intoxicated may not be capable of consent.
3.  Alcohol is involved in most campus crimes; if you choose to drink, please practice legal low-risk drinking.
4.  Trust your instincts; if you feel uncomfortable with friends or strangers remove yourself from the situation.

threat to other students and employees described in paragraph (1)(F) that are reported to campus security or local law police agencies. Such reports shall be provided to students and employees in a manner that is timely, that withholds the names of victims as confidential, . . .

. . . and that will aid in the prevention of similar occurrences.

## OUR SUGGESTED LANGUAGE

### Crime Alert 1

[City] Police state that a male acquaintance reportedly sexually assaulted a female student at an unidentified fraternity house in _____ in the early morning hours on Thursday, August 25, 2016.

### Crime Alert 2

[City] Police report two sexual assaults in recent days.

1. A male acquaintance, identified as a [University] student, reportedly sexually assaulted a female in the early morning hours of Sept. 9 in an outdoor area in the _____ block of _____ Street. No description of the suspect was provided.
2. A male acquaintance reportedly touched a female student inappropriately and refused to stop. The incident reportedly occurred at a bar in the _____ block of _____. The student identified the male, and police are investigating.

### Crime Reduction Tips:

1. Consent is required for all sexual activity. Consent is active, mutual, enthusiastic, conscious, and ongoing participation in sexual activity by all individuals.
2. According to Ohio law, sexual assault includes any unwanted sexual activity obtained through force, threat, intoxication, or authority.
3. Actively debunk rape myths. Sexual assault is about power, control, and privilege, one person feeling entitled to violate another person. 1 in 5 women survive rape on college campuses, and 27% experience unwanted sexual contact. Men can be victims. Anyone, regardless of sex, gender, sexuality, or gender identity, can commit or experience sexual assault. 80% of perpetrators are friends, classmates, dates, or partners—not strangers. False reports of sexual assault are very rare (less than 2%, according to FBI statistics), about the same rate as other crimes. Victims do not falsely report in order to get revenge. Violence is never the victim's fault.
4. If you experience sexual assault, it is your choice whether or not to report it. If you do report it, please understand that university faculty and staff are required to share that information with the dean of students and others on campus. Confidential sources—who are not required to report—are available in the university counseling office and through local advocacy organizations. You may take advantage of campus support services without reporting the crime to police.

*Figure 3. Comparison of language in the Clery Act, our university's crime alert, and our suggested language.*

As shown previous page, the Clery Act does not require the specific language used by our institution in the crime alerts. Our suggested language both conforms to federal law and provides an accurate, survivor-centered, just response. It is clearer and less blaming both in describing the crimes and in defining terms. While our university does not in fact define either consent or sexual assault, our suggested language does so concisely and in accessible terms. It also makes clear that at our specific university (though not everywhere; this is an institutional decision), faculty and staff have mandatory reporting obligations—a key fact that may influence a survivor's decision to disclose, and to whom.[12] Importantly, instead of emphasizing the presumed dangers of underage drinking, we highlight some of the most common and pernicious rape myths, using the crime alert not just as a reporting tool but also as a way to educate the campus community proactively.

## CONCLUSION: REFRAMING JUSTICE

As we have shown, university crime alerts can either contribute to rape culture and victim blaming on campuses, framing consent as murky or ambiguous, or they can work to dismantle rape culture and foster a clearer, more just theory of consent. One difficult truth for universities is that reporting requirements, such as those included in the Clery Act, do not have an impact on campus incidents of sexual assault: rates of sexual assault on campus have shown no signs of decline since these laws took effect (Anderson 2016). Although our university (following Clery) frames its response in terms of "Crime Reduction Tips," the fact is that reducing crime—in particular crimes rooted in oppression, such as sexual assault—is a difficult, if not impossible, task, and certainly reporting crime alone does not sufficiently lower the incidence of violence. Safety is, in many ways, an illusion, and one that only (ironically) serves to perpetuate fear and ignorance. What universities *can* do, however—and what we maintain they *must* do—is to create a campus climate that centers the experiences and dignity of survivors, and that aims to deconstruct rape myths and rape culture while reconstructing justice according to nonviolent principles. Crime alerts ought to function as part of that important work, not as a barrier to it.

How, then, ought we to (re)conceptualize justice? We insist that justice is worldmaking: cultivating a more feminist campus, where sexual assault is neither ignored nor blamed on victims or underage drinking, but instead where a radical critique of rape culture and a survivor-centered, healing-centered culture of student dignity, autonomy, and community can flourish. While campus crime alerts constitute just one piece of that culture, they do send a powerful message to the campus community about whose dignity the campus values and what kind of campus we want to cultivate. This includes recognizing—rather than minimizing or denying—the prevalence of sexual assault on college campuses and fostering a community educated about consent, rape culture, and victim blaming. Finally, it includes constructing a community that responds to survivors with radical belief, support, respect for their agency, and available resources for healing.

The necessity for college campuses to provide a counternarrative of justice rooted in feminist and antiviolent principles is urgent in a culture where Brock Turner's violence was dismissed and normalized by the justice system, his family, and mainstream media reports, all mobilized in protection of his future, and where women who add their voices to the Me Too movement face blaming and shaming (as well as violent threats) as a result (see Gilmore 2017; Manne 2018). What would happen if—instead of mobilizing to support Turner—the justice system, parents, and mainstream media reports had instead surrounded the woman he raped with support, belief, and outrage? What would happen if her powerful statement, which she read to him in court, became required reading at colleges and universities across the country, and if campus actors in charge of sexual assault reporting—not just in Title IX offices or in advocate roles, but also deans of students, heads of counseling services, and authors of crime alerts—were educated about advocacy-based concepts of consent and survival?

Survivors themselves provide the clearest, most powerful ways of reframing justice, a fact reflected in the language of our suggested alerts as well as the language we use throughout this book.[13] We end this chapter with the final paragraph of the letter one survivor read to Brock Turner in court, openly defying a system that had defined justice in terms of his future rather than hers:

And finally, to girls everywhere, I am with you. On nights when you feel alone, I am with you. When people doubt you or dismiss you, I am with you. I fought everyday for you. So never stop fighting, I believe you. As the author Anne Lamott once wrote, "Lighthouses don't go running all over an island looking for boats to save; they just stand there shining." Although I can't save every boat, I hope that by speaking today, you absorbed a small amount of light, a small knowing that you can't be silenced, a small satisfaction that justice was served, a small assurance that we are getting somewhere, and a big, big knowing that you are important, unquestionably, you are untouchable, you are beautiful, you are to be valued, respected, undeniably, every minute of every day, you are powerful and nobody can take that away from you. To girls everywhere, I am with you. Thank you. (Baker 2016)

We must turn to survivors for a clearer understanding of consent, for language that will serve to empower and support, for knowledge of what campuses need to foster healing and education, and for ideas about how to theorize justice as worldmaking.

## CHAPTER 2

# STEPPING UP IN A SAFE HAVEN

## CRITIQUING CAMPUS CONSENT INITIATIVES

Consent has become big business. As universities struggle to comply with federal laws addressing campus sexual assault prevention, many have placed their trust in online training programs designed by corporations and organizations that define consent for students and claim they can personally reduce sexual assault incidents on campus. These one-size-fits-all, corporate-style trainings turn consent education into a purchasable product. One such program, Step Up!, describes itself as a "prosocial behavior and bystander intervention program" that educates students in its five-step method: "*Notice the event; Interpret it as a problem; Assume personal responsibility; Know how to help; Implement the help—Step UP!*" (Step UP! 2018).

In this chapter, we argue that while such outsourced campus initiatives might provide an easy way for universities to achieve compliance, they are rife with problems, especially the assumption that individual students' taking "personal responsibility" to intervene is the best answer to the problem of sexual assault on campus. As our analysis shows, such a construction of individual students as personally responsible for either avoiding sexual assault or intervening when it happens fundamentally misconstrues violence as an individualized problem and proactively puts responsibility for violence on victims and bystanders—not the violent person. Ultimately, we recommend that universities avoid outsourcing (purchasing) consent initiatives and instead engage students in an ongoing, analytical educational conversation about consent and violence that questions cultural norms about gender, gender identity, and sexuality and that takes advantage of campuses' own expert faculty and staff.

Increasing awareness of sexual violence in the press, in popular culture, and among higher education administrators and professionals—in addition to pressures from lawmakers, parents, alumni, and donors—has resulted in a number of these initiatives aimed at teaching students about consent and sexual assault. Many such programs target new and incoming students—those perceived as most vulnerable to committing or experiencing sexual assault because of their newness to college life and supposed inexperience with independence, substance use, and opportunities for sexual activity; other programs include peer education efforts that reach students throughout their educational journeys (whereby, for instance, a trained group of students visits a meeting of a student organization or a class to give a panel presentation). Other resources and opportunities exist, such as student groups and campus-wide events for Sexual Assault Awareness Month in April, but participation in these programs is self-selected—whereas programs for new students, and to a lesser degree, programs that occur within student groups or classes, may better reach all students, even those without a particular interest in understanding or preventing sexual violence.

This chapter analyzes the Haven online sexual assault prevention program and the Step UP! bystander education program, two national brands implemented on our campus, as well as a training session led by a staff person from Everfi, the company that sells the Haven program among other corporate trainings. We acknowledge our university's effort to reach new and continuing students with important messages about obtaining consent and preventing sexual assault; however, from a critical feminist and queer theoretical perspective, we contend that these programs have a number of major problems. Specifically, we argue that as fiercely individualist corporate programs, Haven and Step UP! largely obscure social and community responsibility for consent (including the cultural contexts of power and oppression in and through which consent is constructed), exemplify and buttress the neoliberal university, and promulgate paternalistic assumptions about women in particular (specifically young White women). By constructing consent as a matter of individual choice and personal responsibility, by framing consent in (hetero- and cis-) normative terms, and by conceiving of education as akin to corporate training, these programs contribute to the regime of neoliberalism in higher education that we critique throughout this book. Moreover, our analysis demonstrates the insidious alliance between neoliberalism and normativity. "Trainings," which construe universities as corporations and students as consumers to satisfy and protect from harm, work to produce ideal customer-citizen-subjects whose relationships, sexualities, and gender identities fit into prescribed (and marketable) categories.

By outsourcing consent education rather than drawing on the expertise of faculty, universities that hire Haven and Step UP! provide a one-size-fits-all, factory-assembled training model that markets itself as an efficient way to achieve federal compliance with Title IX and the Violence Against Women Act (VAWA). The "training" model, based on corporate diversity and sexual harassment trainings that are shown to have dubious effectiveness at best (Dobbin and Kalev 2016; McGregor 2016; Vendantam 2008), suggests a vocational skill to be learned and mastered, rather than a body of knowledge that requires academic courses, the input of scholars, and critical reflection across time. Meanwhile, any problems with the trainings—such as the use of normative or exclusionary language and examples—can be excused as not the university's precise responsibility, even as the problems are replicated in schools nationwide. Finally, programs such as Haven and Step UP! rely on the problematic assumption that a quick, one-time online training will suffice to educate students about consent and sexual assault, when they have potentially received a lifetime's worth of inaccurate and harmful (mis)information about those topics. In other words, we argue that these campus initiatives do more to protect the university from liability and preserve its reputation in the public eye than they do to educate students. We suggest that a more effective approach to consent education would involve the university faculty (and possibly staff) across all of a student's college years in in-depth, cross-curricular critical thinking about gender, sexuality, and cultural constructions of agency, relationships, and ethics. We are not suggesting adding to faculty's already heavy workloads, but instead building consent education into the curriculum. Such an approach to consent education would—like consent itself—be ongoing.

We hope our critiques of Haven and Step UP! will inspire more effective, inclusive, and sustained consent education. Before undertaking a close reading of the campus consent initiatives at our university, we offer a critique of research about best practices for teaching students about consent.

## WHAT IF THEY DON'T CONSENT TO LEARNING ABOUT CONSENT?: REACHING STUDENTS WITH CONSENT INITIATIVES

Campuses have not only a legal responsibility to teach students about consent, but also a moral responsibility (it is the right thing to do) and a pedagogical responsibility (universities exist primarily to teach). Despite this triune responsibility, universities have not always embraced the task with enthusiasm, and when they do, they often sidestep the moral and pedagogical. Instead, universities frequently prioritize their own reputations and compliance with legal requirements, as we also show in chapter 1 (see also, Marine and Nicolazzo 2017).

The ubiquitous use of the term *training* to describe efforts to educate students about consent represents, in a nutshell, the extent to which neoliberalism and normativity infuse these efforts. Training, or its cousin "programming," connotes a corporatized moment of skill-building that employees and good-corporate-subjects can use to perform their jobs more effectively (i.e., generate more revenue). This language ought to sound alien in a university context, where terms like "education" or "curriculum" should be more familiar. Kenneth Burke (1966) contended that language serves as a terministic screen, reflecting reality in specific ways, selecting particular details to emphasize, and deflecting less-desirable aspects of a subject. We submit that the ease with which universities employ such language reflects the neoliberalization and corporatization of the university, selects a view of students as primarily consumers, and deflects universities' ostensibly pedagogical raison d'être.

If universities embrace their duties only reticently, students' eagerness to learn about consent is sometimes no better. Several studies have found that men in particular resist learning about consent because they perceive training programs about sexual and interpersonal violence as accusatory (Foubert 2011b; Foubert and Cremedy 2007; Kilmartin and Berkowitz 2005; Rich et al. 2010). Even programs that do not critique toxic masculinity and that leave the fundamental tenets of the gender binary in place may fail because many men students reject the message out of hand. In response to this problem, scholars recommend framing training more carefully to focus on (1) the social construction of toxic masculinity (Kilmartin and Berkowitz 2005; Rich et al. 2010); (2) what it feels like to experience assault (to generate empathy and reduce rape myth acceptance) (Foubert 2011b; Foubert and Cremedy 2007); and (3) how men can intervene presumably to protect the women in their lives from potentially assaultive situations (Carlson 2008; Foubert 2011b; Foubert and Cremedy 2007).

Programs that last a whole semester or have a degree of repeated contact over time have worked more effectively than one-off trainings (Anderson and Whiston 2005; Barone, Wolgemuth, and Linder 2007). Studies have mixed results about the efficacy of peer education versus trainings conducted by professionals (Anderson and Whiston 2005; Foubert 2011b; Foubert and Cremedy 2007). Required trainings reach more students but have less buy-in from students, whereas optional trainings likely only reach the students least in need of the message (Kilmartin and Berkowitz 2005; Rich et al. 2010); even so, voluntary trainings help campus staff to identify potential student leaders (Kilmartin and Berkowitz 2005). Trainings that include research on campus norms can help dispel myths about the number of students on campus who drink regularly, find sexist jokes funny, and feel entitled to sex; telling students that a majority of other students reported they would intervene if they witnessed an assault may help empower students to step in when they otherwise might feel social pressure to mind their business (Kilmartin and Berkowitz 2005).

One fairly consistent argument in the research on educating students about consent advises sex segregation in programming. While one meta-analysis found that men fare no better in segregated training compared to co-ed trainings (Anderson and Whiston 2005), other studies and programs argue that men feel less accused and safer to ask questions in trainings with only other men present (Foubert 2011b; Foubert and Cremedy 2004; Kilmartin and Berkowitz 2005). John Foubert developed the most well-known examples of sex-segregated trainings, as well as many of the findings in support of sex-segregated training. He describes his "Men's Program" and "Women's Program" as "the only program in the scholarly literature shown to reduce sexual assault among men" and "one of the only programs shown to increase bystander behavior among women," respectively (1).[1]

Foubert's program for men, designed to be presented in about an hour by a team of speakers, focuses exclusively on helping men understand how to support women who disclose an experience of sexual assault. Ostensibly to increase men's empathy, the program includes a clip of a police training video in which a heterosexual, man police officer, in the process of moving trash bins in an alley, is accosted by two heterosexual men with a gun. The men rape the police officer, which the trainer frames as an act of power and dominance rather than sexual desire. The officer worries about contracting a sexually transmitted infection and faces incredulity from his colleagues when he returns to the police force, with some of his coworkers gossiping that perhaps he enjoyed the encounter or had met the men before (Foubert 2011b). The program for women, by contrast, focuses on bystander intervention and features a video of a police interview with a rapist who describes how he targets victims; the training hopes to teach women about warning signs to notice in the men around them. (Presumably, women are not already aware of such warning signs and need to learn how better to protect themselves and their friends.)

We dwell on Foubert's programs because, while they are backed by an impressive amount of (Foubert's own) empirical research,[2] we have concerns about the politics of the Men's Program and the Women's Program. Published critiques of Foubert have focused on his claims of uniqueness and his methods of assessing effectiveness; however, the political assumptions of his approach remain unquestioned (for critiques, see Berkowitz 2002; Tharp et al. 2011; for responses, see Foubert 2002; Foubert 2011a).

One of our concerns with all sex-segregated programming (and most of the research about it), including Foubert's, is the degree to which such programming minimizes the needs, concerns, and perspectives of lesbian, gay, and bisexual (LGB) students and completely erases the lives and experiences of transgender (including nonbinary) and gender-nonconforming students on university campuses. Indeed, it is unclear where some students might locate themselves in the rigid gender binary of the Men's Program and the Women's Program. Research on LGB students has found that gay and bisexual men experience similar rates of sexual assault on campus as heterosexual women; bisexual women experience sexual assault at nearly twice the rate of heterosexual women (Ford and Soto-Marquez 2016; Pino 2016). "Sexual assault of transgender persons," write Kosenko, Rintamaki, and Maness (2015), is "disturbingly common" (3; see also Stotzer 2009). More than 29 percent of trans and gender-nonconforming students report experiencing sexual assault during their college years (Marine and Nicolazzo 2017; Pino 2016). While quite a bit of research considers the problem of sexual assault of trans folks in prison (Campbell and Holding 2015; Iyama, 2012), much work remains to understand more fully the experiences of trans folks on campus, particularly related to sexual violence (but see Marine and Nicolazzo 2017; Wyss 2004). In short, queer and trans students, especially queer and trans students of color, stand at increased risk for sexual assault, so we find fault with any training whose content or form presumes, relies upon, and exacerbates cisnormativity and heteronormativity—particularly because research has found that campuses more inclusive of lesbian, gay, bisexual, transgender, and queer (LGBTQ) students tend to have fewer incidents of sexual assault than campuses less welcoming to LGBTQ students (Coulter and Rankin 2017).

In addition to its cisnormativity and heteronormativity, the Men's Program and its framing of consent also rely on and buttress hegemonic masculinity (see Trujio 1991). Even if we were to acknowledge the program's empirical successes, we must ask: At what cost? By promoting the training as a way to help "good" men learn how to "protect" the presumably defenseless women around them, the program depends on a paternalistic understanding of gender roles according to which women need the help and protection of men. Like the trite expression "she's someone's sister, someone's mother, someone's daughter," which neglects that "she" is, in her own right, *someone*, programs that teach men how to protect women also promote men's dominance and masculinist values—values that precisely denigrate women. If, as many studies agree (Carlson 2008; Coulter and Rankin 2017; Kilmartin and Berkowitz 2005; Rich et al. 2010), the problem of sexual violence on campus comes from structurally supported and systemic toxic masculinity, we aver that addressing the problem requires a critique of hegemonic masculinity, not an approach to education and programming that both draws from hegemonic masculinity's tenets and contributes to its perpetuation.

In addition to the paternalistic framing of the Men's Program, the primary source of this program's success has been traced to the police training video that describes a man's rape at the hands of two other men. The video makes clear that all three men identify as heterosexual and are romantically coupled with women. In Foubert's (2011b) view, mentioning the men's heterosexuality in the video and repeating it in the presentation inoculates against homophobic interpretations on the part of the audience, and presenters repeat this defense if asked about the potential homophobia of the video during the question and answer period following the presentation.[3] However, we contend that because compulsory heterosexuality and homophobia constitute fundamental components of hegemonic masculinity, the mere assertion that none of these characters identify as gay does not preclude homophobic implications. Part of the horror for the man in the video is the suggestion by those around him that he knew the men who raped him, that he met them before, and that he enjoyed the assault. In many ways, such hurtful remarks from a survivor's friends, family, and coworkers comport with the experience of heterosexual women who survive rape. But for a straight woman, the idea that she has attraction to (some) men and desires sexual activity with (some) men does not, in itself, constitute a source of shame or a threat to her femininity. Indeed, she may even have felt attraction to her attacker and have had consensual relations with him in the past. Of course, previous consensual sex is used to blame women survivors regularly, but nonstraight men survivors are uniquely shamed and blamed for their attraction to men. Illustrating the Men's Program's rather thin conceptualization of the politics of homophobia, Foubert offers this defense of the video as an example response for presenters to use during a talk:

> A common manner in which homophobia manifests is assuming that if a man is raped, his attacker must be a homosexual man. The video we use describes a situation in which a man is raped by presumably heterosexual men, thus helping debunk the myth that men who rape men are necessarily homosexual. In addition, we hit this point home immediately after the video concludes by noting that the perpetrators were presumably heterosexual, as with many male-on-male rape situations. Thus, we work to attenuate homophobia, not perpetuate it. Also, think about this for a second. Many programs for women have focused on describing women being raped and the effects rape has on them, but these programs surely don't perpetuate misogyny and violence against women just because they talk about women who are raped. In the same way, our program does not perpetuate homophobia, we actually do the opposite. (Foubert 2011b, 101)

As tidy as this answer sounds on a superficial reading, a closer look reveals some shaky arguments. The final claim quoted above conflates misogyny and homophobia, and while homophobia and sexism certainly relate to and mutually inform one another (Pharr 2014), making them consubstantial does a disservice to both. Foubert's answer here also erases gay men and queer and trans folks who experience rape. No part of this response addresses the homophobic shame heaped upon the man victim. We concede that the training's allusion to the homophobia implicit in the shame the officer feels references a real problem for men who experience sexual assault, but the training leaves the homophobia unmarked. Moreover, by erasing gay men and queer and trans people, the program also leaves out an analysis and critique of forms of coercion unique to LGBTQ folks and relationships, such as threatening to out someone or top/bottom coercion.

Our critique of Foubert stems not from quantifiable conclusions about his programs, but rather from a critical queer and feminist understanding of sexual violence. We affirm that quantifiable results alone ought not constitute the highest value in sexual violence education and prevention work. Campuses have a responsibility to educate students about consent and violence in a way that is emancipatory, not one that trafficks in homophobia or that relies on exclusively heteronormative and cisnormative framings of sexual violence, victimhood, and agency. As we turn, then, to a critique of our own university's attempts to teach incoming students about consent, we do so informed by previous research on consent trainings but also by a feminist, queer, and transcentric critical lens (Spencer 2014). The personal—indeed, the interpersonal—is political, and we contend that efficacious training must comport with an epistemology and axiology of emancipation from all forms of oppression. Understanding violence prevention as separate from feminist and queer critique is not only inaccurate but also perpetuates oppression and therefore violence. To examine consent training with a critical lens that understands consent as radical respect for students' boundaries means, for us, centering the experiences and needs of survivors: especially women students, queer students, trans and gender-nonconforming students, and students who occupy these identities simultaneously with other marginalized positionalities.

## HAVEN AND STEP UP!: A CLOSER LOOK AT ONE CAMPUS'S TRAINING EFFORTS

At our university, all incoming students must take an online training program called Haven. Failure to complete the training blocks students from registering for courses. The training includes modules on sexual assault and interpersonal violence. It begins with an acknowledgment that sexual assault and interpersonal violence affect everyone (for those who have not directly experienced such violence, the training module says, "chances are you know someone" who has). Students take a pretest that asks what they would do in hypothetical situations as well as how they predict a majority of students at the university would act in the same circumstance. The pretest also asks students about their own experiences with "unwanted sexual contact," and the directions clearly indicate that the questions are anonymous and will not be reported to the university. The next section focuses on personal values and asks students how they apply their values in interpersonal relationships. The training explains warning signs in relationships and includes example scenarios. Students then need to "e-sign" to indicate that they have read the university's sexual harassment policy (linked as a PDF document). Haven gives students general definitions and university-specific definitions for terms like sexual assault and stalking. In the following section, students are asked to think about their strongest communication skills, and then to reflect on how they could use those skills if someone were to confide in them about experiencing assault, or if they were to hear a sexist joke or see a situation that could lead to rape, such as a house party where someone seems to be plying another person with drinks in order to take advantage of her.

In the section focused specifically on consent, students must indicate, on a five-point scale from "yes" to "no," whether various nonverbal codes mean consent to sex in an imagined scene between Damien and Jackie (laughing, kissing, touching someone's arm). The section presents a few more hypothetical situations and asks students to brainstorm ways to intervene, for instance, if a friend of theirs planned to get someone drunk at a party in order to take advantage of them. Haven then concludes with a campus-specific video in which several constituencies of students take the "It's on Us" pledge to end sexual assault. The video includes representatives from our university's Greek organizations, sports teams, the student body president, and the presidents of the College Republicans and College Democrats.

Many aspects of the Haven program align with best practices for online training (Lynch 2002). Participants must click quite a bit in order to finish, since it includes several activities, quizzes, and surveys that require engagement with the material presented before moving to the next screen. Several screens include text that a student could click past without reading, but Haven has enough screens requiring some interaction that students have to engage with at least some of the material. The content of the training quietly includes different races and sexual orientations. Images and speakers in videos and examples reflect different racial and ethnic groups, and several of the example scenarios include gay and lesbian characters or relationships. The opening survey allows multiple options for gender identity and sexual orientation, including a blank line for students to enter an identity not included. On the whole, definitions are easy to understand and apply. The training makes explicitly clear in many places that targets of sexual and interpersonal violence are not to blame. Haven actively debunks some rape myths (such as stranger danger). The training explains the steps for reporting incidents, includes campus and national norms from survey data, and offers a range of bystander intervention strategies.

However, Haven also has serious limitations. Besides one statistic about the greater incidence of sexual assault among gay and bisexual men (compared to straight men), no information in the training is specifically tailored to gay, bisexual, and lesbian students, and no information appears about race and ethnicity. The mere inclusion of characters of different races illustrates what Jodi Melamed (2006) has theorized as neoliberal multiculturalism, wherein signifiers of racial inclusion function to mask the deeper racism at work in neoliberalism (see also, Ahmed 2012; Spencer and Patterson 2017). Transgender and gender-nonconforming students are not mentioned. Although Haven nominally rejects victim blaming, it also subtly engages in some blaming rhetoric, especially in the section on stalking, which places responsibility on targets to tell their stalkers to stop. Other parts of the training betray paternalistic assumptions, as in a positively-presented example of bystander intervention where a student in a video explains his rationale for verbally objecting to sexism from group members during a class project: he assured viewers he was "not trying to be the thought police" but decided to intervene because "what if someone said that about your sister?" (The ubiquitous victimized woman or girl family member appears whenever trainings need a reason to oppose sexism.) Beyond content, the form of the Haven training has some navigation weaknesses, especially when university-specific information appears. In all cases where university documents and definitions follow Haven's more general explanations, the information appears in aesthetically banal blocks of text that participants can easily skip, except when the system requires students to "e-sign." In these cases, students may click past without reading everything, even though the local, customized information arguably holds more relevance for them.

While we accept the basic premise that all students (incoming and otherwise) ought to be educated about consent and university policy, we remain troubled by the online training model as well as by some of Haven's assumptions that go unstated and uninterrogated. In chapters 1 and 5 of this book, we discuss Sarah Deer's (2015) conceptualization of rape as a community wrong. As a corollary to that position, we argue that consent is a community responsibility. As a ruthlessly neoliberal program, Haven deflects social and community responsibility for consent by putting the onus on each individual student to seek consent in their own relationships and interactions and to take action if they see a classmate in a potentially dangerous scenario. For example, asking students to intervene in social situations where they witness abusive or potentially assaultive behavior relies on an individualist model of intervention. As an online training, Haven lends itself to isolation; nearly all students will take Haven alone, and probably as quickly as possible. Unless students have a chance in a class or student organization to discuss the content (far from guaranteed), they may never think through the content presented, let alone consider how consent is communally constructed and how violence affects specific communities. Certainly consent involves decisions by individuals, but those decisions never happen in isolation.

To provide a contrasting example, we have both completed mental health trainings available on our campus. Part of the process involves engaging in role-play exercises where workshop participants take turns asking each other "Do you think you might hurt yourself?" or "Have you felt suicidal?" Recognizing the difficulty of talking about suicide and self-harm, the workshop presenter asked us to practice so that we could hear ourselves saying the words, watch our interlocutors' facial expressions, and respond to their answers. Having a safe opportunity to practice these skills has served us well in actual conversations with students in crisis. Haven's closest parallel only requires students to click a button in a multiple-choice quiz about what they might do in a tense situation, and anyone who has taken a test before can reasonably guess which of the choices likely counts as the "correct answer" (the most socially desirable choice).

We also believe that such individualist framing works insidiously to confer responsibility for outcomes on bystanders and victims rather than perpetrators. As Rebecca Solnit (2016) argues, the erasure of the masculine perpetrator in neoliberal rhetoric, seen everywhere from the Centers for Disease Control's drinking guidelines for women to schools' girl-focused dress codes, contributes to the erasure of masculine responsibility. But the responsibility should not therefore shift to the (presumed masculine) bystander. Certainly the solution to victim blaming is not shifting responsibility to bystanders; doing so perpetuates victim blaming rather than challenging its hegemony. Just as someone who stays sober and alert and "does everything right" can be assaulted, even the most aware bystander who intervenes in all the recommended ways may not be able to protect all of his friends. Further, encouraging students to be ever-vigilant in stopping crime recalls other problematic contexts, such as neighborhood crime watches and Homeland Security "see-something-say-something" messages, which can easily lead to discriminatory profiling and policing of other students.

In other words, Haven's brand of individualism displaces rather than defuses potential harm. Much like trainings that focus on women's defensive strategies, those that center the potential intervention of bystanders risk shifting responsibility for sexual assault (to the student with less awareness, or the student whose friends do not intervene). Trainings should teach intervention skills (in ways that are not paternalistic),[4] but fight, flight, or freeze responses to trauma may occur for bystanders as well as for someone directly experiencing trauma.

Online training programs such as Haven emerge from a corporate context in which federal requirements create a market for trainings as prepackaged products. Everfi, a company that specializes in training programs for schools and businesses, owns Haven. In 2014, Everfi reported that more than five hundred colleges and universities use its training products, and in the fall 2013 semester alone, more than four hundred thousand students from 196 different institutions nationwide took the Haven training course (Everfi 2014). (Everfi also offers training about financial matters, corporate responsibility, and sports—true entrepreneurs and consummate capitalists, indeed.)[5] As we suggest above, outsourcing training programs to for-profit companies like Everfi, rather than drawing on university women's centers and expert faculty, ensures that students receive minimal, one-size-fits-all trainings that fail to address the complexity of consent and violence and that do not adequately reflect specific university cultures, policies, and concerns. Instead of reflecting critically on the power dynamics of the university or the culture at large, students are encouraged both to individualize instances of assault as outside the norm and to be ever-vigilant for when it inevitably occurs. Meanwhile, universities outsource responsibility for consent education to a corporation in order to achieve compliance with federal law. As we argue in chapter 1, such neoliberal policies construct student-consumer subjects who are deemed "good" or "bad" based on individual behaviors, choices, and even purchases.

The danger of making consent education into a product is evident outside of the training as well. Kimberley Timpf, Senior Director of Prevention Education at Everfi, visited our campus on April 18, 2017, and presented a talk called "Campus Briefing on Student Alcohol Use and Recommendations for Progress," wherein she argued that national and campus-wide conversations about sexual assault need to address alcohol more directly and seriously.[6] She presented national data as well as data based on our students' responses to alcohol use surveys. Most of the talk focused on ways to reduce "risky" drinking, conflating alcohol use with sexual assault. Timpf noted that alcohol functions as a major barrier to reporting of sexual assault because survivors who use alcohol commonly blame their drinking for the assault. This self-blame only worsens when peers weigh in. She went on to argue that because alcohol affects everyone's ability to express desires, feelings, and needs, sexual assault under the influence is no one's fault. She followed up this baffling claim with an example scenario where Rob and Erin, two hypothetical university students, have a conversation while drinking. Timpf's slideshow included Rob and Erin's speech and thought bubbles. Rob invites Erin back to his room, and Erin says, "I'll come back with you but can't stay long." When she says this, she means she just wants to hang out briefly before she leaves (according to her thought bubble). But Rob's thought bubble indicates that he feels certain Erin's acceptance of his invitation means she wants to have sex. Timpf asserted that when Rob discovers that Erin actually does not want sex, he may turn in his frustration to more aggressive behavior, because of the influence of alcohol. "The communication here," lamented Timpf, "isn't clear."

In our view, Timpf has presented a situation that is quite clear, one in which nothing about Erin's response communicates that she wants sex. The responsibility for "clear communication" here, ostensibly distributed equally, is constructed as entirely on Erin. In Timpf's view, Erin's agreement to come to Rob's apartment for a short time justifies his expectation for sex. Could we imagine this same scenario reversed, such that we blame Rob for poor communication because he never says, "When we get back to my place, I'm going to pressure you for sex even though you said you didn't want to stay long"? Linguist Susan Ehrlich's (2001) analysis of the language of rape trials critiques the historical practice of the utmost resistance standard, which recognizes an act as rape only if the victim resists to the utmost; under this standard, if the victim gives up fighting back at any point, the act is presumed consensual. U.S. jurisprudence in the twenty-first century has abandoned the utmost resistance standard, but it still exists, lurking around in the guise of "the miscommunication model of date rape" (121). For someone who represents Everfi to blame rape (an act of entitlement and dominance) on a combination of alcohol and miscommunication is especially dangerous. As Kilmartin and Berkowitz (2005) explain, poor communication may contribute to the risk of sexual assault, but "sexual assaults result from one person imposing their wishes on another. Strategies for improving communication assume that both parties have equal power, which is not the case in situations leading to sexual assault" (89). Timpf's egregious error here casts doubt on the credibility of Everfi and its product, Haven. Although Haven does not have a similar misstep, the fact that the company's representative gave a talk for campus administrators and student services personnel that endorses a miscommunication model of sexual assault invites questions about Haven. Has Everfi conducted research and kept up with best practices from feminist, survivor-centered perspectives, or does their profit motive mean they will hire anyone, regardless of how poorly trained and prepared?

In addition to Timpf's misunderstanding of assault and alcohol, Everfi's "Campus Briefing on Student Alcohol Use" also constructs students in moral terms: "good" students (presumably women) either don't drink, or make the choice to "drink responsibly"; "bad" students do not—and look what can happen. Likewise, "good" students (presumably "good men") intervene when they witness violence; "bad" students do not. In this way, Everfi draws on a neoliberal discourse of responsibility and personal choice to make sexual assault a problem of alcohol consumption and to construct normatively gendered student-subjects who are either vulnerable (women) or strong and protective (men).

Trainings such as Haven are infused with the norms and discourses that characterize mainstream campus culture. As scholars and teachers, we must ask: Who benefits from misunderstandings of sexual assault as a problem of alcohol use and/or miscommunication? No approach to consent education that subordinates consent to substance use will build the kind of world we imagine. Rather than radical respect for boundaries, Timpf advocates for clearer, soberer communication—a move that does not take consent seriously and that absolves rapists of blame for their violence.

One of the limitations of Haven is that students can complete it in a couple of hours and never think about it again. Ongoing exposure to messages about consent presents more hope that students will remember what they have learned and apply those lessons in practice. The Step UP! program offers one way of continuing the lessons about consent from Haven. Like Haven, Step UP! is a national program that different campuses implement in localized ways.

Step UP!—a program cosponsored by the National Collegiate Athletic Association (NCAA), developed by athletic and student affairs staff, and heavily marketed to athletic directors and coaches—focuses exclusively on bystander intervention, not only in cases of (potential) sexual violence, but also in other situations, such as alcohol poisoning, gambling addiction, depression, discrimination, disordered eating, hazing, and academic dishonesty. Step UP!, in other words, takes the "if you see something, say something" aphorism and turns it into a national educational effort that buttresses neoliberal ideology in colleges and universities around the country. Not only does the prevention of sexual assault become the responsibility of each individual student on campus—for Step UP!, one focus is not enough. Individual students, through their diligence and radical embrace of personal responsibility, can solve any number of problems that plague themselves or their friends. Structural and social factors that contribute to sexual assault, alcohol poisoning, gambling addiction, disordered eating, and academic dishonesty get downplayed throughout the resources, examples, and scenarios on the Step UP! website. Of course, that follows logically from the program's purpose: it exists to train people to intervene in potentially harmful situations. While bystander intervention training can embrace a communal understanding of consent, its underlying assumptions deserve interrogation. It encourages masculinist protectionism as well as affirming the gender binary. As we show above in our critique of Haven, it also individualizes the problem of sexual violence as one of "personal responsibility." Moreover, it presumes that individual bystanders will always be rational actors, when cases such as George Zimmerman's unjust shooting of Trayvon Martin show that cultural bias (including racism and other forms of discrimination) plays a key role in identifying a problem and deciding what to do about it. Finally, to what degree does a program like Step UP! serve to insulate university athletics and the NCAA from their responsibility in contributing to a culture that excuses rapists, foments disordered eating, and reproduces discrimination?

One of our concerns about Step UP! is its myriad topics. Is a one-size-fits-all bystander intervention training an adequate response to such vastly different problems (discrimination and hazing)? Moreover, if Step UP! functions as one of the few ways for students to learn more about consent or even to refresh what they learned in Haven, we fear the wide variety of topics distracts from its usefulness in educating students about consent. At best, Step UP! seems to prefer breadth over depth, but to whose benefit, and at what risk?

The sexual assault page of the Step UP! website includes five sections: scenario, questions, definitions and consideration, action steps, and resources. The scenario asks the reader to imagine attending a party and observing a man friend talking to an intoxicated woman, giving her drinks, and then walking upstairs with her, though "it is clear that the woman has had too much to drink." The questions invite the reader to consider how they might react if the woman were the reader's sister or mother (here we go again!), then ask how athletes are acculturated, what masculinity and femininity mean, and whether society offers contradictory messages about sex. Question 9 seems worth quoting: "Are there sexual assault cases currently in the news and what lessons are to be learned?" In both its syntax and its politics, that question is misguided. Without offering context, interpretation, or possible answers to these questions, Step UP! allows for any number of interpretations, some of which work against the goals of challenging rape culture and creating a more livable world. As even cursory attention to any news story about campus sexual assault reveals, a number of people who see coverage of athletes (and others) accused of sexual assault take the side of the accused, demonizing the victim (Manne 2018). Blogger Julie Sprankles (2016), for instance, humorously collected headlines about the Brock Turner rape case that emphasized his swimming career rather than his crime and minimized the seriousness of his violence. Annie-Rose Strasser and Tara Culp-Ressler (2013) compiled several examples from the rape case in Steubenville, Ohio: CNN called the assailants "promising students" whose lives would be ruined by their rape convictions, while ABC placed the blame on new technology (the rapists in this case had filmed their crime), and NBC focused on the harm that would befall the rapists because they now have to register as sex offenders. Academic researchers have shown how feminist activists use social media to create a counterpublic that speaks back to the rape culture regularly perpetuated by mainstream media coverage of sexual assault (Boux and Daum 2015; Patil et al. 2015; Salter 2013; Sills et al. 2016). Thus, when Step UP! asks what lessons an athlete can learn from cases of sexual assault in the news, we observe that the "lesson" someone takes from current events may differ markedly from what a reader of the Step UP! website should come away knowing.

Though the website offers no correct answer to this or any question, the "considerations" section that follows the questions speaks to the issue of media coverage directly:

> While there is little consistent data to suggest that athletes commit these crimes more often than non-athletes, numerous mediated events around the issues of sexual assault have recently focused on athletes. Media focuses [*sic*] on the high profile athlete because they are considered "newsworthy." (Step UP! 2018)

The website, then, sanctions an answer to question 9 that delegitimizes victims' narratives in cases where athletes get accused. Notice the scare quotes around the word *newsworthy*. In the parlance of Step UP!, athletes' newsworthiness registers as dubious, perhaps unfair; after all, "there is little consistent data to suggest that athletes commit these crimes more often than non-athletes." Step UP! ignores that athletes' newsworthiness emerges from their already existing national profile. Here, the media get blamed for a persecution campaign against athletes when in fact the athletes' status renders them newsworthy figures regardless of whether they commit any crimes or are accused of any.

The sentence that follows troubles us further: "With that said, it is very important as team members that athletes engage in appropriate sexual boundaries, Step UP! and intervene in an effort to decrease the incidences of sexual assault within our own communities." In other words, athletes ought to practice bystander intervention (branded as "Step UP!") because otherwise, media crusaders will target them with negative publicity. Intervening in a violent situation becomes a brandable product wielded to avoid bad press, rather than a thoughtful decision requiring reflection on specific contexts and circumstances. Where, we wonder, does consent come in? Does consent matter to Step UP! and the NCAA, or do they just aspire to avoid lawsuits and bad press for their athletes?

In press coverage highlighted on Step UP!'s website, this concern for protecting athletes at victims' expense is echoed again in an article about Acadia University's football team. One team member opines, "One guy does something wrong . . . and everyone assumes the worst.

We wanted to protect the team." One of the coaching staff, meanwhile, says he is "proud of the number of players who stuck it out over 20 weeks and the overall personal growth that resulted" (Nova News Now 2017). While we are not against athletes' "personal growth," we are against constructing consent training as a way of "protect[ing] the team" or prioritizing athletes' growth over victims' healing.

If one can forgive the questionable framing and motives of the website, the action steps do offer some useful tips about believing survivors and a clear (if scanty) definition of consent ("Consent is hearing the word 'yes.' It is not the absence of hearing 'no.' It's the LAW!"). The action steps provide correctives to common rape myths, such as stranger danger and false reporting. They also acknowledge that while men may experience sexual assault, "the majority of sexual assault cases involved male perpetrators and female victims." But the initial framing blames media instead of perpetrators for making sexual assault cases newsworthy. The action steps tell us to believe victims, but should we believe them if they appear on the local or national news because their attacker plays a key position on the football or basketball team? At what point do we move from the sound advice in the "action steps" into the paranoid framing of the "considerations"? Anytime an athlete finds himself accused, or only when he ends up on the news?

In addition to these concerns, Step UP!'s sexual assault page offers no material specifically related to LGBTQ students, and even the passing acknowledgement that men can experience sexual assault offers no information about sexuality. Gender identity is completely absent. LGBTQ students already experience disproportionate alienation on athletic teams (Halterman, Gabana, and Steinfeldt 2017), a reality only compounded for those who also experience sexual assault. This notable absence is particularly unfortunate.

## CONCLUSION

In 2016 Annie Clark and Andrea Pino built on the work they chronicled in their documentary *The Hunting Ground* (2015) by publishing the book *We Believe You: Survivors of Campus Sexual Assault Speak Out*. Their contributors—of several races, genders, and gender identities—detail harrowing experiences, not only of sexual assaults ɔut also of ineffectual campus responses, lenient (if any) ɔs, and the ongoing trauma of continuing to share campus their attackers. Observing the common threads in many ɪeriences, Clark and Pino (2016) reflect on a question they often hear now that they are antiviolence advocates: "High school students and, even more often, their parents ask us, 'Which colleges are really the bad ones?' or 'Which campuses are rape free?' or 'How rapey is this place?,' as if there's a way to avoid going to a college where sexual assaults occur. As far as we can tell, people are sexually assaulted on and around every college campus" (26).

Without naively supposing that sexual violence is fully preventable, we suggest that campuses can fulfill their pedagogical and ethical imperative (as well as their federal mandate) to educate students about consent and construct campuses less rooted in rape culture and more steeped in radical respect for students' boundaries. Campus education initiatives are necessary but not sufficient for that work. We submit that campuses ought to begin with the *politics* of their educational initiatives, not with minimum standards for satisfying federal statutes.

Educational programs that begin with a politics of consent as radical respect for boundaries ought to focus on the lives and experiences of survivors, especially those students most vulnerable to assault—not just by population, but by proportion as well. Simply stated, education programs must actively resist centering the experiences of cisgender students. Trans and gender-nonconforming students' experiences must have a central place (not *the* central place, but *a* central place). Trans and gender-nonconforming students must not find themselves symbolically annihilated (as they are in the programs we analyzed in this chapter) or merely tacked on as a marginal or peripheral footnote to an otherwise cisnormative program. In their fascinating interviews with sexual violence prevention educators at universities around the United States, Marine and Nicolazzo (2017) identify the ideal type of programming as "gender transformative" (14). We echo their call, with the understanding that gender transformation is not achievable in a single online training program.

Therefore, consent education must be ongoing. It must actively work to resist rape myths, victim blaming, the miscommunication model of sexual assault, the utmost resistance standard, protectionist models of masculinity, gender stereotypes and the gender binary, and other common handmaidens to rape culture. Well-intentioned buttressing of rape culture foments hostile campus environments for survivors and works to make life less livable. As we show in our analysis of Step UP!'s website, sound advice loses credibility if its writers first frame it as a way to avoid media persecution rather than a way to live ethically.

Instead of promoting normative models of consent and violence, consent education should work to make clear the links between sexual violence, acceptance of rape myths, and toxic masculinity (Chapleau and Oswald 2014; Hockett et al. 2009; Posadas 2017) and between violence, capitalism, racism, and imperialism (Davis 1981; Deer 2015). Violence arises in contexts of power imbalance and oppression, so working to change those power dynamics is the best way to construct cultures of consent. Educational initiatives rooted in a radical notion of consent, axiomatically, work to untangle normativity rather than prop it up. They also simultaneously engage in a critique of neoliberalism. Consent ought to be a community value, not just an individual behavior; consent's opposite, violence, is a community wrong, not merely a personal transgression. Consent matters because it is ethical, not because it is required by law, or because it is marketable or profitable. Our approach to consent education would be at odds with the gender-segregated approach presumed to be most effective, such as Foubert's Men's Program, and it would certainly be at odds with the neoliberal corporatespeak of Everfi and Step UP!. But, we argue, such programming would be more effective—and by "effective," we mean that it would contribute to a more just world.

## CHAPTER 3

# CONSENT GOES VIRAL

## SEARCHING FOR POSITIVITY IN ONLINE MEMES

The viral video "Consent: It's Simple as Tea," a 2015 collaboration between Emmeline May and Blue Seat Studios, has been widely circulated on social media and taught in high school and college classrooms as well as advocacy trainings. It features simply drawn stick figures who dramatize consent in black and white. Likening sexual consent to the act of agreeing to tea, the video presents consent as a "simple" concept with clear and obvious meanings: if you offer someone tea and they say no, do not force them to drink tea; and if they pass out before finishing the tea you have offered, do not force them to drink it while unconscious. In the video, what is often considered murky and complex, with lots of gray area, is presented as basic: literally black and white. However, when it comes to consent messaging, what seems simple and obvious is often laden with mistaken (and normative) assumptions. In the "Simple as Tea" video, one person is the tea *maker*, and the other is the tea *drinker*; one is active and one passive—no other configurations of power or relationship are represented. In real life, of course, many sexual encounters do not match this active-passive configuration. Thus we must ask, as we do throughout this book: how is consent constructed?

To address that question in this chapter, we turn our focus to consent messages that take the form of viral Internet images, cartoons, or videos. Collectively, we refer to these messages as *consent memes*, drawing on a capacious understanding of the term *meme*. As Limor Shifman (2013) defines it:

> In the vernacular discourse of netizens, the phrase 'Internet meme' is commonly applied to describe the propagation of content items such as jokes, rumors, videos, or websites from one person to others via the Internet. According to this popular notion, an Internet meme may spread in its original form, but it often also spawns user-created derivatives. (362)

In analyzing consent memes, we make no claims about the empirical effects of exposure to these messages or about the representativeness of the examples in any statistical sense. Instead, we argue for a sort of qualitative analytical generalizability, to invoke a phrase from Jimmie Manning and Adrianne Kunkel (2013). By attending to messages about consent that we have seen in various contexts on our own social media feeds (largely populated by feminist scholars and activists), as well as in training events, workshops, and feminist blogs, we show how even largely praiseworthy and progressive messages about consent risk reifying harmful messages and stereotypes. Even where we might endorse a message about consent, we often feel troubled about the sex negativity in many consent memes. So in addition to the questions we pose above, we wonder if progressive, antirape-culture messages about consent can also have sex-positive possibilities.

## THE RHETORICITY OF MEMES

In the last two decades, memes have emerged as a cultural force, and more recently, as objects of critical attention by rhetoricians. Millions of people have watched viral videos such as "Leave Britney Alone" or "Numa Numa," catapulting their creators from obscurity to fame, including appearances on late night talk shows, parodies in other popular media, and sometimes a brand of their own (Burgess 2008). Most memes do not reach viral status, but they nevertheless function rhetorically to inform, persuade, or entertain as they circulate among social networks and blogs.

Memes, writes Christopher Duerringer (2016), "serve as a significant means of political consciousness building" (9), and as such, rhetoric scholars have called for more research (Davis, Glantz, and Novack 2016; Hahner 2013; Johnson 2007; Shifman 2013). Among visual arguments, memes stand out because of the ways they are shared and adapted in and among social networks (Davis, Glantz, and Novack 2016; Duerringer 2016; Hahner 2013; Huntington 2016). By their very nature, memes require participation; their rhetorical force depends on the extent to which viewers modify and/or share them. To attend to memes, then, is to recognize the increasing importance of analyzing content generated not only by powerful elites, but by everyday Internet users as well (Kuznekoff, Spencer, and Burt 2017).

Beyond analyses that point to the usefulness of memes for rhetorical critics and the appropriateness of memes as objects of study, other articles have posited that memes as a form or mode demand a different kind of analysis than singular, static texts. Eric Jenkins (2014) refers to memes as a mode, explaining that "Modes are collective, emergent phenomena that express the circulating energies of contemporary existence rather than re-presenting the interests of particular rhetors" (443). As such, critics ought to consider not just "specific rhetors and audiences" but also "the virtual relations established between rhetors, texts, and audiences as they interface with memes" (443). For Jenkins, no one actualization of a meme can represent or explain the meme in its entirety, so although examples are helpful and necessary for analysis, the larger goal should be not a deeper understanding of any individual instantiation of a meme, but instead an appreciation for the work of the meme-as-mode. Attending to memes in this way acknowledges the speed of images and visual arguments too often neglected by analyses that treat images as (only) historical (DeLuca 2006; Johnson 2007). Elucidating the importance of accounting for the rhetorical force of images' speed, DeLuca (2006) writes:

> In the ceaseless circulation of images in our media matrix, speed annihilates contemplation, surface flattens depth, flow drowns moments, distraction disrupts attention, affect eclipses

meaning, the glance replaces the gaze, reiteration erases origi-
nals, and the public screen displaces the public sphere. (87)

DeLuca's observations seem especially to apply to memes because
memes move among potential viewers when shared on Twitter,
Facebook, Tumblr, blogs, and other social media platforms. Content
rapidly spreads to multiple feeds, where viewers usually scroll quickly,
often reading only headlines, not clicking links, and sometimes sharing or commenting before reading the content (at all or in full) (Dewey
2016). "To read photographs," DeLuca warns, "is to skew them into
objects palatable for the print gaze" (88).

However, we suggest that memes are not *only* impermanent,
multiple, and superficially read. Memes also "stick," and "stick around,"
in ways that have profound effects on creators, adapters, and viewers.
Social media preserves even specific iterations of memes, allowing
them to be more than glanced at over time. Moreover, the reiteration of
a meme over time in different ways does not necessarily mean there is a
lack of depth or meaning; rather, we argue that memes have a life cycle.
For the purposes of our analysis, we look to a few particular examples of consent memes that have "stuck around" for several years, but
our goal transcends the singular and bounded task of analyzing given
messages. We also look toward patterns and trends in contemporary
consent memes, and, crucially, we imagine other possibilities. Perhaps
to DeLuca's disappointment, we gaze rather than glance, but without
jettisoning his important observation that audiences do indeed glance,
at least some of the time. Our analysis of three consent memes reveals
patterns that contribute to an overall understanding of both consent
and sexual activity as negatively constructed—that is, these memes
define consent by what it is *not* rather than by what it *is*. Thus, even
when these messages aim to resist rape culture (and in some ways suc-
ceed), they come with some troubling entailments as well. Our analysis therefore invites reflection on how to communicate consent from a
sex-positive point of view. To us, sex positivity means promoting the
sexual freedom and wellbeing of all individuals, especially marginalized ones, *as well as* the need to interrogate socially constructed and
heterosexist oppressive sexual norms—because, as bell hooks (2015)
puts it, "re-thinking sexuality, changing the norms of sexuality, is a
precondition for female sexual autonomy" (148).[1]

## SEARCHING FOR POSITIVITY IN CONSENT MEMES

In this section, we offer a rhetorical analysis of three consent memes: a cartoon, a public service announcement campaign, and a video. Each of these texts does important work in defining and conceptualizing consent for students and other audiences, including dispelling several myths popularized by rape culture's hegemony. Alongside the strengths of these memes, however, we also demonstrate how their conceptualizations of consent depict it only in the negative, that is, by what it is *not*. While we acknowledge that it *is* important to showcase examples of nonconsent for students and others, we also insist that consent messaging and memes ought to include examples of consent in action. We conclude our analysis by reflecting on possibilities for more positive, and sex-positive, understandings of consent.

### Everyday Consent

In "What If We Treated All Consent Like Society Treats Sexual Consent?," a colorful cartoon posted on the website *Everyday Feminism*, artist Alli Kirkham cleverly explains sexual consent through a series of apt analogies.[2] The cartoon—shared more than 175,000 times from the *Everyday Feminism* website alone—features several three-panel narratives, each unrelated to the others, with a diverse set of characters of various skin tones and gender expressions. The cartoons position the characters in prosaic settings in which interlocutors somehow violate their consent. One narrative features two White characters, one man-appearing and one woman-appearing. She allows him to borrow her car in the first panel, and in the second panel, he shows up to take the car the following week; when she objects, "You can't take my car whenever you want it!," he retorts, "That's bullshit! You said I could have it once so I should be able to have it all the time." In another narrative where both characters are wearing tank tops and gym shorts, one character continually hands the other a set of weights. Finally, the heavy-laden character says, "I don't want to carry this stuff." The response back: "Well, you're dressed like a weightlifter and showing off your muscles. You're asking to be handed heavy stuff! Don't blame me." The other narratives include someone who plays a friend's favorite song for her (but while she was trying to sleep), someone who expects his spouse to make breakfast every day because she made it one day, and someone who decides after learning the rules of poker that she would rather not play the game after all, among others.

Much in this cartoon deserves praise. Kirkham places common excuses for sexual assault and several victim-blaming tropes of rape culture in the mouths of man-appearing, woman-appearing, and androgynous-appearing characters and creates a sense of what Kenneth Burke (1959; 1984) calls perspective by incongruity by decontextualizing these tropes from sexual assault. Of course, the title of the comic strip makes the analogy clear. The absurdity of expecting to borrow someone's car anytime because one borrowed it once, or forcing someone to play poker because they went through the trouble of teaching it, stands in contrast to rape culture's normalization of victim blaming, not to mention the notion that people in established relationships (especially marriage) can just expect sex. In many ways, these different narratives dovetail nicely with our own understanding of consent as respect for boundaries, particularly because the comic highlights the boundaries we take for granted as fixed (such as not playing loud music while someone sleeps). Several of the narratives include the passing of time ("the next morning," "a short time later," "the next week," "1/2 hour later"), a move that reflects sensitivity to the idea that consent is best understood, in the parlance of Kelly Oliver (2016), as a process rather than a moment (indeed, one character's misunderstanding of this fact underscores much of the tension in each narrative). Also worth noting: Kirkham acknowledges that consent matters in all manner of relationships and demographic arrangements; the cartoon does not reproduce the man-as-aggressor/woman-as-victim trope so common in communication about consent. Indeed, the gender expressions across the panels undermine the cisnormativity of many consent messages—even while no characters' gender identities are explicitly marked, the variety of gender expressions at least implies that consent matters in trans relationships, too. For all these reasons, we support the use of this cartoon as a way of explaining consent, especially when it stands alongside other nuanced considerations of consent.[3]

What this cartoon sets out to do, it accomplishes with aplomb. However, we also observe that the cartoon always imagines consent in terms of clearly bifurcated agents, where one person transgresses and the other person reacts. The reactive characters do stick up for themselves in every case, asserting their agency, but sometimes only after their consent has been violated (the character whose friend tattoos him while he is unconscious stands out as the most extreme example, but the person awakened by loud music illustrates this as well). In other cases, the offending character has the last word, so the audience does not know whether the reactive character's boundaries remain intact. For instance, one narrative involves a character who invites his friend to watch *Pulp Fiction*. The friend decides after thirty minutes that he does not wish to finish the movie, to which his host replies, "No! You said you'd watch the movie so you're staying until it's done." The host also reaches his arm across his friend's chest, as if to block him from leaving. Whether he is forced to finish the film is up to the viewer's imagination, but regardless of the outcome, the bifurcation is clear.

Moreover, taken as a whole, this cartoon defines consent negatively, that is, by what it is not. We learn that to consent to something once does not mean consent any time, that how someone dresses does not imply consent, that sleeping or unconscious people cannot consent, and that consent at one moment in time does not imply or replace the need to obtain ongoing consent. However, we do not get a sense of what consent actually looks like. As important as we regard the message about avoiding nonconsent, we insist that messages about consent ought also show what consent *can* mean and what positive, ongoing, and enthusiastic consent looks like. We recognize the unfairness of expecting this cartoon to do more than it aims to do, and as we already noted, its work in unmasking rape culture's treachery deserves admiration. What is troubling is not so much this singular actualization of a viral consent message that defines consent negatively as the pattern it seems to exemplify.

### Don't Be That Guy

To offer another example, consider the "Don't Be that Guy" campaign by the Sexual Assault Voices of Edmonton (SAVE).[4] The campaign featured a series of public service announcements (PSAs) with a single image and a two-line sentence that often begins "It's not sex . . ." and concludes with an example of nonconsent. The campaign logo appears in much smaller print at the bottom of each ad. One PSA (fig. 4) shows a woman and two men in a men's bathroom (a urinal in the background clarifies the setting). The woman seems to be struggling to stand up, and the two men on either side of her have their hands on her back and waist. "It's not sex . . . when she's wasted," the copy reads. A single sentence below the main copy explains: "sex with someone unable to consent = sexual assault." Another ad shows two men from the shoulders down, seated on a couch. The man on the right has his hand on the other man's leg, while the man on the left appears to be pushing his interlocutor away. The text reads: "It's not sex . . . when he changes his mind." And below that: "sex without ongoing consent = sexual assault."

This campaign, too, does worthy work in defining and demystifying consent as well as challenging rape culture. It offers several different scenarios where someone cannot or does not consent, including sleep, unconsciousness, intoxication, mind changing, and refusal; it includes one same-sex pairing, illustrating that consent matters beyond heterosexual relationships; and it represents situations where the people targeted for assault know their potential attackers: these men are in their cars, homes, or public places, and as we note throughout this book, assaults by acquaintances, friends, and romantic partners are far more common than those by strangers in dark alleys.

On the other hand, this PSA series reinscribes the man-aggressor trope (ossified in the campaign's title "Don't be that *Guy*"), figures consent as an active/passive binary, and again, tells us what consent is not. While the vast majority of gender violence is perpetrated by cis men,[5] campaigns that represent a monolithic image of perpetrators risk further alienating survivors who face incredulity if their experiences do not fit the cultural script of sexual assault. Because of this campaign's negative definition of consent, we might learn what kind of guy not to be, but not what kind of guy *to be*. The campaign also erases the woman's agency entirely. Unlike in the cartoon by Kirkham, this campaign features single images where the decision about what to do next seems entirely left up to the (aggressing) guy. He can choose to keep going or stop; to get the intoxicated woman home safely (and then what?) or not;

to pressure someone or to lay off. This PSA campaign, then, for all its advantages, illustrates the same pattern as the *Everyday Feminism* cartoon in enacting a pedagogy of consent defined negatively—teaching viewers what consent is not and erasing victims' agency. SAVE's website lists several organizations that have used the campaign and makes it freely available to distribute, provided the group using the campaign agrees not to alter the images. Although it is laudable to disseminate messages about consent in this way, we wonder what gives these negative understandings of consent such rhetorical force. In other words, we ask if these memes are doing some positive cultural work that is nonetheless ultimately limited by a negative framing of consent.

### Consent as Tea?

One consent meme commonly seen and taught is the "Consent: It's Simple As Tea" video mentioned in the opening of this chapter (fig. 5). Not only has this video made its rounds on social media feeds, but we have also seen it at conferences and in presentations from sexual assault prevention advocacy experts, including on our campus. The video has been viewed more than two million times on YouTube alone. The Step UP! program, which we analyzed in chapter 2, even includes "Consent: It's Simple As Tea" as one of the first linked resources on its webpage about preventing sexual assault. As we noted above, the video presents consent as a matter of black and white—literally. Two stick figures (drawn in black) interact on a white background, while a masculine-sounding voice narrates. The color red appears in a few places in the video, usually to draw a "no" symbol (as in "no smoking") over a cup of tea to reiterate that someone who declines or who has passed out does not want tea. We appreciate the clarity of this video. Moreover, the video is a valuable pedagogical tool, for both its strengths and its shortcomings. As stick figures, the characters have no apparent sex or gender expression and so can stand in for anyone. The metaphor works in the same way as the other consent memes analyzed here to upend some of rape culture's assumptions; for instance, the idea that once people get sexually aroused, they reach a point of no return is addressed by the video's reminder that someone may agree to tea and decide later not to have it, or may start drinking tea but pass out before finishing it, or may decide not to drink the rest.

*Figure 4. Sexual Assault Voices of Edmonton, "Don't Be that Guy" Campaign.*

The tea maker never has a right, avers the video, to watch someone finish a cup of tea just because of the work put in to make it.

But the tea meme also relies on a tea maker with agency and a tea drinker (or refuser) who is mostly passive. This meme, like the others, offers a negative understanding of consent as something someone may decline to give or withdraw at any time. And the masculine voice that narrates the video could be understood as (yet another) example of consent mansplained. Moreover, the tea metaphor does little to address oppression (for example, the privilege one person can wield in a relationship due to gender, gender identity, nationality, or race), and its "simple as tea" slogan fails to acknowledge the legal complexities of rape and other forms of sexual assault, the increasing acceptance among legal and advocacy workers that pressuring and other forms of emotional coercion can be considered forms of violation (Ybarra and Mitchell 2013),[6] or the larger question of how to build respectful relationships in a sexually dysfunctional culture. Finally, the "Consent is Like Tea" video has been critiqued for trying to make sexual assault funny and for condescending to college students and other common audiences (Young 2015; National Union of Students 2016).

In posing the question *what can consent mean?*, we want to imagine how this video might communicate largely the same metaphor about consent but in a sex-positive way that understands consent as a mutually derived rhetorical and relational construct. What if two people worked together to fill the kettle, turn on the stove, select the tea (maybe even mutually agreeing on new flavors once in a while), add the milk and sugar, and stir the tea? Along the way, both tea makers can check to be sure the other person still shares enthusiasm about the direction the tea is taking, and they can do likewise when the time comes to drink the tea. They can wait together for the tea to reach the right temperature to drink, and warn one another with safewords if it turns out a sip of tea they thought they were ready to enjoy is too hot and thus painful. Of course, some people like their tea to burn their tongues a bit, so if both parties are in mutual agreement, especially hot tea may be welcome for one or both. Our tea drinkers may feel hospitable enough to invite others to join them for tea, and in that case, as long as everyone involved is continually enjoying the tea, we say, brew on.

Our reimagining of the tea metaphor understands sex in an ideal way—as a positive and enjoyable experience that people share—and consent as a mutual, ongoing process that is relationally constituted. Here, both enjoyable sex and its prerequisite, consent, are shared responsibilities and joys in the context of the couple's (or group's) interaction. This expanded and more sex-positive metaphor also accounts for group sex and kinky sex, and we observe that kinky sexual

*Figure 5. A Screenshot from the YouTube Video "Consent: It's Simple As Tea."*

subcultures have a rigorous set of ethical standards and consent guide-lines, including the use of safewords, practices of discussing desires and expectations before sexual activity, and aftercare, all of which may serve to enrich larger conversations about consent, including by chal-lenging normative definitions of consent (Bauer 2014). In addition to offering a sex-positive way of thinking about and communicating about consent, this extended metaphor recognizes that consent means more than *not* forcing sex on someone or *not* taking advantage of a passed-out acquaintance. Consent—including sexual consent—also means attending to emotional needs and boundaries before, during, and after a sexual encounter. Of course, such an ideal may not always be possible for many people, given the ways in which oppression func-tions to constrain individual desire and autonomy. But consent memes might include ideal sexual encounters anyway, to encourage viewers to rethink sexual norms and to help enable a less oppressive future.

## CAN SEX-POSITIVE CONSENT MESSAGES GO VIRAL?

DeLuca (2006), Johnson (2007), and Jenkins (2014) each call the atten-tion of rhetorical critics to images qua images, particularly with respect to the speed at which images move and circulate, and ask us to consider the rhetorical force of images at which audiences glance rather than gaze. We have argued, conversely, that memes can have staying power and are rhetorically and pedagogically valuable as a result. But to glance (or gaze) at any of the consent memes we have analyzed here is to learn about consent negatively, through what it is not. Despite the achievements of these texts in talking back to rape culture, they risk conveying a limited view of sexual activity. Of course, to talk about nonconsent is to talk about violence, not sex—and these memes correctly insist that all of us should avoid committing violence. Here lies our essential argument: while nonconsent is (about) violence, *consent is about more than avoiding violence.* Consent ought to be about more than a paralyzing fear of doing something wrong. Consent is a gift we give and receive communicatively in a relational construction of mutual, radical respect for others' boundaries and needs. While we argue throughout this book that consent defined in this way is constrained by heterosexist oppression (as well as other forms of oppression and privilege), creating and sharing consent memes that offer examples of such consent is surely one way to foster sexual freedom and justice.

How to communicate consent in the temporal register of memes may seem vexing. In one sense, memes represent a particularly neoliberal kind of technology, as fully privatized messages that rely on market logics to spread. Only the most entertaining or provocative will circulate broadly (Shifman 2014). While John Michael Roberts (2014) argues that new and social media can increase feelings of connection between citizens and their elected leaders, even participatory forms in the age of the Internet find themselves shaped by the forces of neoliberalism (Fenton 2011). As we have shown, consent memes that reproduce logics of individualism, while valuable, miss the richness and depth of consent as we understand it. But, we aver, other possibilities for imagining consent, even in the form of memes, exist. Images and their viral circulation may indeed be fast and getting faster, but consent ultimately hinges on recognition of self and other as whole and dignified. Consent means co-constituting, cultivating, understanding, and respecting boundaries. As a process, consent is and must be slow (compared to a moment), thoughtful, and relational. How might such a concept translate into a mode of seeing in which "speed annihilates contemplation, surface flattens depth, flow drowns moments, distraction disrupts attention, affect eclipses meaning" (DeLuca 2006, 87)?

As we have argued throughout this chapter, the adaptability and rapid spread of memes does not necessarily result in a loss of depth or meaning; rather, in their reiterative movement, they have a rhetorical and pedagogical function that makes them worthy of critical attention. Our analysis has aimed to identify the patterns of meaning-making in contemporary consent memes. Beyond offering correctives to extant memes, such as our expansion of the tea metaphor above, we wonder if creative consent advocates and instructors may benefit from embracing what Joshua Trey Barnett (2015) calls *temporal pedagogy*. In his analysis of trans man Joshua Riverdale's blog, Barnett shows how Riverdale chronicles his transition process with a series of monthly photographs that show his body's development on hormones. In contrast to emergence narratives of trans identity (think Maury Povich's before-and-after episodes), Riverdale's blog illustrates transition as a slow evolution. As such, "Riverdale's photographic sequence instructs viewers to see and understand the (transsexual) body as a site of fleshy metamorphosis" (Barnett 2015, 164). Barnett goes on:

> To suggest that Riverdale's photographic sequence offers viewers a way of seeing and understanding the transsexual body as a fleshy site of "becoming with" is to argue that it works against dominant logics of the body as an immutable, bounded entity. (165)

How might we think about consent in an analogous way? If we understand consent as a process of "becoming with," we also work against hegemonic understandings of consent as boundedly negative, as a hortatory *no*. Reimagining consent from a starting place of sex positivity and with attention to all consent can be(come) requires temporal pedagogies of consent: memes that even in their speed ask all of us to slow down, relate, and co-constitute better relationships and worlds.

## CHAPTER 4

# TRIGGER WARNINGS AS HOLISTIC CONSENT

## A SOCIAL JUSTICE RATIONALE

O n August 24, 2016, *The Chicago Maroon*, the student newspaper at the University of Chicago, tweeted a photo of a letter the class of 2020 received from college dean Jay Ellison. The letter congratulated new students on their admittance, then informed them about the university's "commitment to freedom of inquiry and expression." According to the letter, this commitment "does not mean the freedom to harass or threaten others" but *does* mean that "we do not support so-called 'trigger warnings,' we do not cancel invited speakers because their topics might prove controversial, and we do not condone the creation of intellectual 'safe spaces' where individuals can retreat from ideas and perspectives at odds with their own" (O'Dowd 2016). Ellison's letter goes on to encourage students to read a book he enclosed with the letter, *Academic Freedom and the Modern University* (Boyer 2002), which details the "history of debate, and even scandal, resulting from our commitment to academic freedom."

The letter's tone unmistakably suggests that Ellison feels proud of these scandals surrounding academic freedom, but the letter invites several questions he never unpacks or explores. If, indeed, freedom of expression does not mean freedom to threaten, might a warning about potentially trauma-triggering material in a reading or film prevent a threat to a student's wellness? If freedom of expression does not mean freedom to harass, would the university uphold its commitment not to cancel lecture invitations to speakers known for legitimating violence against women (Bill Maher), committing violence against women (Bill Cosby), or naming and advocating the rape of particular people in the audience (Milo Yiannopoulos)? Does the concept of "safe spaces" in fact provide students an insular refuge against new ideas? The letter also suggests, "Fostering the free exchange of ideas reinforces a related University priority—building a campus that welcomes people of all backgrounds." As nice as that sounds, does that mean the university would support a professor who invites a White supremacist to speak to a social movements class, in a misguided effort to balance the perspective of a Black Lives Matter speaker? As a White man, Dean Ellison may not feel unsafe in the presence of such speakers, but his privilege means he never has to think about his safety. It therefore may be easy for him to dismiss so inaccurately the notion of intellectual safe space as carefully theorized and practiced by feminist scholars and our allies for decades.[1]

In this chapter, we take up these and other questions, prompted by Ellison's letter and the many responses to it in mainstream media discourse and peer-reviewed journal articles. In Ellison's letter, we see in brief many of the common arguments and misunderstandings of those against trigger warnings, but we endeavor here to do more than offer a rebuttal. Instead, we pose this question: *What can trigger warnings do?* We argue that the fierce public and scholarly debate over trigger warnings in university classrooms has often characterized the issue as one of academic freedom and ignored the social justice arguments for trigger warnings. We suggest that rather than limiting speech, trigger warnings actually expand academic speech by engaging students more fully in their own learning. Our view centers a holistic understanding of consent, to include students' rights to intellectual, emotional, and physical boundaries—by which we mean (at a minimum) freedom from undue or preventable trauma. By framing trigger warnings as a social justice issue and a matter of consent, we argue that faculty ought to imagine trigger warnings as tools of worldmaking to the degree that they promise to improve accessibility, engage students better in learning, and cultivate more just and livable campuses.

## A SERIES OF STALEMATES: THE CURRENT SCHOLARLY DEBATE ON TRIGGER WARNINGS

Trigger warnings have inspired considerable debate in recent years, often connected to a dubious critique of the so-called millennial generation as more sheltered, coddled, or easily offended than generations before. A number of key arguments circulate and recirculate, resulting in what we see as a series of stalemates.

The first matter of importance, as always, centers on the work of definition. What is a trigger warning? In our view, many of the misunderstandings and misconceptions about trigger warnings begin here, where some assume they require faculty members to allow students to opt out of class discussions or to avoid readings with which they disagree or that make them feel uncomfortable. Erica Goldberg (2016), for instance, writes, "Students must learn to engage with those who disagree, and should understand that not being affirmed is not the same as being ostracized" (752). Although Goldberg frames her argument as one against trigger warnings, no serious advocate of trigger warnings would suggest that they apply to anything or everything with which a student disagrees. Instead, trigger warnings are statements that alert students about material that may provoke the reliving of past trauma. As Eleanor Lockhart (2016) explains, the name "trigger warning" comes from the established concept of trauma triggers in clinical psychology, where a trigger refers to something that causes clinical symptoms, especially but not exclusively for people experiencing posttraumatic stress disorder (PTSD).

The often repeated argument that trigger warnings "coddle" students and discourage learning about difficult or challenging material relies on this crucial definitional misunderstanding (Carter 2015). In their survey of psychology faculty, Boysen, Wells, and Dawson (2016) found that many faculty had negative views of trigger warnings; however, the qualitative comments of those who disapproved of trigger warnings revealed that what they actually objected to was the idea of offering students a way to avoid dealing with course material, which is not in fact what trigger warnings do. Furthermore, these same faculty regularly offered behavior warnings (such as reminding their students not to self-diagnose on the basis of one class) and even content warnings (before discussing suicide)—so they rejected trigger warnings in theory but actually appeared to use them without recognizing it.[2]

To examine another example, in their widely read article published in *The Atlantic*, Greg Lukianoff and Jonathan Haidt (2015) (two men of considerable power and privilege) argue that students have become too sensitive and that instructors who use trigger warnings aim to "scrub campuses clean of words, ideas, and subjects that might cause discomfort or give offense." This misunderstanding of trigger warnings, we argue, is grounded in a thinly veiled contempt both for students who dare to make suggestions about how they might best learn and for mental health in general: "The current movement is largely about emotional well-being . . . it presumes an extraordinary fragility of the collegiate psyche, and therefore elevates the goal of protecting students from psychological harm [and] punishing anyone who interferes with that aim, even accidentally. You might call this impulse *vindictive protectiveness*." Not only do Lukianoff and Haidt seem incensed that faculty might listen to students, but they also scoff at the notion that students' emotional well-being is a valid concern, calling students "fragil[e]" and faculty who consider their needs "coddling," "protective," or even "vindictive."

Like Lukianoff and Haidt, Jack Halberstam (2017) characterizes supporters of trigger warnings as those who "believ[e] in a student or viewer who is unstable and damaged and could at any moment collapse into crisis" (537). And like them, Halberstam both mischaracterizes trigger warnings and minimizes the seriousness of students' experiences of trauma. As Rebecca Stringer (2016) asks, "can we dare to give some ground to students on this question instead of trivialising their concerns?" (64). Logan Rae (2016) calls the dismissiveness of such positions ableist: "The claim that students are 'too sensitive,' rests on ableist assumptions that effectively deny the existence of mental illness and dictate what (re)defines 'real pain'" (96).

The complexity of definition clearly haunts the debate about trigger warnings, as positions that begin with such a thorough misunderstanding of the purpose and scope of trigger warnings often carry those misconceptions into the remainder of their critiques. Nonetheless, one persistent argument that volleys among the pro–and anti–trigger warning camps focuses on whether trigger warnings squelch or expand freedom of speech. Indeed, Ellison's letter (discussed in the opening of this chapter) frames the issue as one of free speech, where trigger warnings (and the like) represent censorship and their repudiation amounts to gloriously unrestrained expression. Whether the right to offer trigger warnings in one's own classroom falls under "free expression" or under behavior "we do not support" is unclear in the letter.

Some of those opposed to trigger warnings highlight the supposed increased reluctance of law school faculty to discuss rape law in their criminal law classes because students might complain about the topic as triggering (Goldberg 2016; Thorpe 2016; Vatz 2016). M. Elizabeth Thorpe (2016) worries, too, that a focus on trigger warnings may have a chilling effect on otherwise organic class conversations: if the day's topic did not come with a trigger warning, but students in class bring up examples or pose questions that move the class in the direction of something potentially triggering, should a faculty member stop the conversation because students have not had the opportunity to prepare for it?

Indeed, no one can know or anticipate all of the possible topics that might trigger students, nor are trigger warnings alone enough to make classrooms radically inclusive (Kafer 2016). The alternative point of view, in favor of trigger warnings, argues that they do not limit free speech, but reflect an adaptation to the reality that the limits of acceptable speech in the classroom have already expanded. Thorpe (2016) explains the latter view:

> In the normative past, topics that might require a trigger warning never would have been discussed. The concerns of people or communities who might be triggered would never be a part of the discussion, or, in some cases, they might never have been members of the audience. The very fact that some believe we might need trigger warnings is indicative of how diversified our speech and audience is now. It is because we have so much more freedom in the topics we bring to the table, and those we include in the discussion of those topics, that

we might need to include a warning when the conversation becomes particularly challenging. (86)

In this view, the sensibilities of students have not softened over the years, but the demographics of student populations have diversified, as has the range of topics considered worthy of scholarly conversation. For instance, in *Academic Freedom and the Modern University* (Boyer 2002), the monograph commended to the attention of incoming students in Ellison's University of Chicago letter, examples of instances where the university defended academic freedom include topics like economic policy and whether reading communist writings amounted to indoctrinating students; by today's standards, these topics strike us as banal, suggesting an overall victory for proponents of academic freedom (in whose number we count ourselves). Trigger warnings ask faculty members not to constrain what they talk about in class, but to let students know when potentially triggering material lies ahead.

Stringer (2016) objects to the notion that trigger warnings allow students to edit course reading lists[3] or skip out on work they would rather not complete; for Stringer, trigger warnings focus not on "*removing* words, ideas, and subjects from the syllabus; instead they are about *adding* a system of warnings or forecasts about upcoming content" (63). By preparing all students for class discussion, trigger warnings work to include more voices in the conversation. As Spencer, Tyahur, and Jackson (2016) have observed, campuses benefit when they consider the conditions that give rise to free expression; classrooms that irresponsibly expose students to trauma, by definition, do not allow for greater expression than those that purposely invite more viewpoints (see also, Kafer 2013, 2016; Spencer 2013, 2017). Regardless of one's stance on trigger warnings, advocates for and against their use seem to agree on the value of academic freedom, including resistance to nonexistent policies that would *mandate* trigger warnings (except perhaps in rare cases where their use comports with federal law under the Americans with Disabilities Act).

One of the more alarming arguments against trigger warnings assumes that exposure to trauma triggers can help people to overcome trauma. For instance, law professor Erica Goldberg (2016) overstates her expertise in assuming that those who experience clinical symptoms need to face their trauma head-on:

> If exposure instead of avoidance is actually better for victims of trauma, a culture of open discourse and dialogue will be altered [if trigger warnings are used] without a corresponding benefit. The art, literature, and films presented in classrooms represent paradigmatic cases of pure speech, where a large part of their value stems from the ability to provoke new feelings and emotions, and creative cognitive dissonance that leads to change. Administrators forcing trigger warnings on professors, in an attempt to nullify the effects of triggering speech, will impose a sterile environment, where feelings are elevated over discourse. (753)

To invoke a colloquialism, we observe that Goldberg's opening line begins with a "big *If.*" Regardless of whether exposure therapy may help a particular individual treat symptoms related to trauma, the college classroom is not the place to receive psychological treatment (from a humanities, art, or law professor, and with twenty-five or fifty other students). Disturbingly, Lukianoff and Haidt (2015) share this assumption that students who have experienced past trauma just need "the thinking cure": "The goal [of education] is to minimize distorted thinking and see the world more accurately. . . . By almost any definition, critical thinking requires grounding one's beliefs in evidence rather than in emotion or desire." These authors' contempt for "emotion or desire" and their belief that trauma in the classroom is equivalent to "distorted thinking" betray a Cartesian bias that severs mind from body and emotion, privileging the mind above all else. In other words, they leave no room for bodies or affect in the college classroom.

Some of the strongest arguments in favor of trigger warnings suggest that their use represents a reasonable classroom accommodation for students with disabilities. For students with a diagnosis of PTSD, warnings for specific trauma triggers may be part of the accommodations students are legally allowed to request, in the same way that students with vision disabilities request larger print materials or students with learning disabilities request extra time on written exams (Lockhart 2016).

Moreover, not all students have a medical diagnosis (something that requires access to healthcare and often multiple expensive visits to medical professionals). For these students, trigger warnings provide access in a way that exceeds medicalized definitions of disability required by universities' disability services offices. Perspectives that frame trigger warnings as matters of accessibility unequivocally rebut the notion that trigger warnings function to prevent offense. In Thorpe's (2016) words, "taking offense is not the same as a panic attack or reliving trauma" (85). Carter (2015) expands on this point at length, highlighting that students who request trigger warning simply ask for "recognition of their lived experiences and institutional support regarding how those experiences influence their education" because "experiences of re-traumatization or being triggered are not the same as being challenged outside of one's comfort zone, being reminded of a bad feeling, or having to sit with disturbing truths."

Alison Kafer (2016) understands trigger warnings as a matter of expanding access to the classroom to more students, with the particular advantage that instructors may choose to give trigger warnings even without having students in their classes who have a particular diagnosis. Indeed, she encourages faculty to think more radically about what access can mean, beyond federal requirements:

> Recognizing that histories of trauma are always potentially present is one way of creating [accessible, crip] spaces; when we conceptualize trigger warnings as forms of access—both *to* difficult material and *for* people with histories of trauma and/ or mental disability—we make room for explorations of how we discuss and respond to those histories. We position trauma and its effects, and our responses to both, as an integral part of our scholarly conversations. (17)

While Halberstam (2017) bemoans what he sees as a "desire to diagnose every neurotic symptom" (537) and Goldberg (2016) regrets universities' "greater focus on mental health and protecting individuals' emotional needs" (738–39)—betraying a fundamental misunderstanding of mental health, if not outright contempt for it—Carter (2015) points out that people living with trauma do not have the privilege of seeing calls for trigger warnings as an excess or a luxury:

> The consideration of trauma in our classroom is not a question of pedagogy or academic labor. It is not about academic freedom, the latest administration of neoliberal policy, or even a debate at all. Teaching with trauma is our daily life.

Uniting Kafer and Carter, then, is a call to conceptualize trauma as an ever-present element of the classroom. Despite the expansiveness of disability perspectives on trigger warnings and access, in practice, as Carter (2015) notes, university policies often individualize trauma in a neoliberal ethic of personal responsibility (and by extension, inadequacy). As Kulbaga and Spencer (2017) suggest, neoliberal frameworks, including self-help and health discourses, often work to limit access even as they purport to expand it (see also, Spencer and Patterson, 2017; Wagner, Kulbaga, and Cohen 2017). Carter's (2015) and Kafer's (2016) commitment to defining trauma more holistically offers the potential to transcend individualized disability approaches that limit notions of access and therefore do as much to reinscribe power relations as to transform them.

To summarize, then, debates about trigger warnings in peer-reviewed journals have focused on their definition (from which other positions seem to flow fairly predictably), their connection to freedom of speech and academic freedom, and their relationship to disability and accessibility. The only consensus seems to emerge on the question of making trigger warnings mandatory, which scholars universally reject except when required by specific disability accommodation requests. (We doubt the importance of this overwhelming consensus, however, because the spectre of university-wide trigger warning requirements seems more fantastical than actual; even universities with policies about trigger warnings do not compel faculty to use them [Lockhart 2016]). Because how one defines trigger warnings seems to predict one's position on their usefulness, we endeavor here not so much to join the debates we have summarized, but to build on them by thinking about trigger warnings as a social justice issue, and specifically as an extension of faculty members' radical commitment to consent, which involves respecting students' intellectual, emotional, and physical boundaries.

## TRANSCENDING THE STALEMATE: TRIGGER WARNINGS, SOCIAL JUSTICE, AND CONSENT

To frame trigger warnings as a matter of consent changes the question from *how should we react to trauma in the classroom?* to *how can we create radically respectful and socially just classrooms?* In other words, we construct trigger warnings as a positive, intentional choice of instructors who commit to creating socially just, consentful classrooms with respect for student boundaries. In the beginning of this chapter, we posed the question: What can trigger warnings do? We suggest, in our more expansive understanding of trigger warnings as one manifestation of a commitment to consent and student wellness, that trigger warnings allow instructors to construct more inclusive classrooms, engage students more directly in their education, and create more just and livable campuses for all students, particularly for students historically underrepresented in higher education.

Trigger warnings can contribute to making campuses and classrooms more socially just by including voices in the conversation that might otherwise remain silent or afraid to speak. If an instructor is open to this idea, they provide a means of cocreating curriculum with students (though we do not believe this is a necessary component). We often invite students early in the semester to make suggestions about the syllabus, and throughout the term we ask them to develop questions in response to course content and participate in discussions when and how they are able. For students without histories of trauma or mental illness, trigger warnings can serve a pedagogical function as well, by modeling how to engage respectfully with a diverse population of individuals with different backgrounds and health needs. They signal to all students that the instructor values their health and wellbeing and does not expect them to perform like automatons without bodies and emotions. For students historically underrepresented in higher education, such as first-generation college students, Pell-grant-eligible students, and gender-nonconforming students, trigger warnings can make college study attainable and enjoyable. And for students with diagnosed or undiagnosed emotional disorders, such as PTSD, depression, or anxiety, trigger warnings can serve as a lifeline in an otherwise hostile sea of abstract ideas.

## Accessibility and Radical Inclusiveness

In contrast to those who reject trigger warnings on the premise that bodily and emotional health have no place in pedagogy (or even that mental illness is fictional), we insist on the reality of mental health—as well as its bodily symptoms and effects—and on the pedagogical value of paying attention to student health and wellbeing. In fact, like Rae and others, we consider many anti–trigger warning arguments to be fundamentally ableist in nature—contemptuous of students and suspicious of the reality of PTSD, anxiety, depression, and other conditions, both diagnosed and undiagnosed.

Disability perspectives on accessibility and inclusiveness, as mentioned in the previous section, are often much more expansive than the legal accommodations available through universities' disability services offices. Disability studies, Kafer (2016) writes, "works to imagine the world otherwise, a world in which disabled people can be seen as desirable, as valuable, as integral" (9). Because legal disability accommodations require students both to obtain a medical diagnosis and to seek out services, they are, ironically, not accessible to all students (including those without access to comprehensive medical care and those who do not identify as people with disabilities). When it comes to mental health and wellbeing, moreover, "disability" may be too medicalized a term to cover every possible instance in which a trigger warning might prove helpful. We argue, then, that what trigger warnings do is to help cultivate radically inclusive classrooms that account for a more expansive range of mental health needs than those more narrowly defined by medicalized discourse.

Radical inclusiveness acknowledges not only the reality but also the range of mental health concerns, which may span "from mild feelings of discomfort to . . . severe visceral response[s]" (Wyatt 2016, 19) to the traumatic symptoms of "students who, if they are triggered, stand to lose weeks recovering" (Stringer 2016, 64). Given this context, for instructors who care about students' needs and experiences, trigger warnings provide one way of expanding educational access to a greater number of students. Such deepened access is particularly important, moreover, for students historically disadvantaged in higher education, who benefit from conceptions of trauma that work against individualized models to acknowledge the politics of trauma. For example, Carter (2015) notes that "the ability to be recognized as a person living with trauma is in many ways a political privilege. Furthermore, while traumatic experiences can certainly be accidental, the vast majority of potentially traumatizing experiences are rooted in systems of power and oppression." A radically inclusive model of trigger warnings includes all students; it does not exclude students without a diagnosed disorder, students of color, nonnormative or nonconforming students, or students who do not identify as having a disorder. Instead, this model helps prepare all students to be more present, intentional, and actively engaged in their learning. And as Stringer (2016) points out, "students who call upon the lecturer to use trigger warnings tend to be also the students who most ardently want the lecturer to teach on that topic that might be triggering for them" (64). Thus, trigger warnings provide a way to make the material more accessible to students—precisely the *opposite* of censorship, the opposite of a threat to academic freedom.

For example, in a 2017 creative nonfiction writing class, trigger warnings allowed for a classroom environment in which students felt comfortable sharing personal stories in writing that included experiences of homelessness, addiction, rape, and attempted suicide. On the course syllabus, under the list of required memoirs we read together as a class, a simply but carefully worded note stated:

> A note about the readings: Authors sometimes write memoirs after surviving or witnessing abuse, assault, family violence, self-harm, military conflict, or other trauma. While these stories are moving and inspirational, they can be painful or triggering to read. Don't hesitate to contact Counseling Services ([number redacted]) at any time, or visit [website redacted] for helpful resources, including suicide awareness and prevention,

> mental health, and veteran support. Self-care is strength!
> Please let me know if there's anything I can do to support your
> learning experience in this class.

Including this note on the syllabus made students aware that the subject matter of the assigned memoirs might require some additional care to navigate. As it turned out that semester, in a class of sixteen students, six went on to identify themselves explicitly as survivors of violence and/ or as having a diagnosis of depression or anxiety. Many of them wrote about those experiences, perhaps because they felt supported and validated in doing so. Perhaps most notably, one student workshopped a beautifully surreal, nonlinear narrative about his suicide attempt after losing his older brother to suicide. Not only did that student choose to stay in the class, complete the readings, and write about his experiences, he also chose to workshop the story with his classmates in order to get feedback to make his story better. To our minds, then, characterizing trigger warnings as "coddling" or "censorship" is a gross misunderstanding of something that ideally includes more students in the learning experience and supports them along the way.

Radical inclusiveness is rooted in a fundamental respect for students, recognizing their full humanity and dignity as physical, intellectual, and emotional persons. Acknowledging that mental and emotional health are pedagogically valid and important also means acknowledging the links between mind and body, or what Carter (2015) calls "bodyminds." Indeed, the term "*mental* health" can be a bit misleading, since the mind and emotions have felt material effects on the body. In the case of PTSD, these can include panic attacks, shaking, headaches, and stomachaches; in the case of depression, these can include muscle pain and lowered energy. In other words, it is not only students' mental or emotional wellbeing but also their physical wellness that affects learning. We make this point not to minimize mental or emotional symptoms, but instead to recognize the holistic nature of trauma and mental health.

### Engaging Students in their Education

Beyond accessibility, we also see trigger warnings as a manifestation of the commitment to holistic consent—respectful of students' emotional, intellectual, and spiritual boundaries—that engages students in their education. By offering trigger warnings, we respect students' agency and dignity by equipping them with a tool that helps them prepare for what lies ahead in the class. In Halberstam's (2017) essay against trigger warnings, he writes,

> the trigger warning boils all explicit material down to assaultive imagery while at the same time it reduces the viewer to a defenseless, passive, and inert spectator who has no barriers between herself and the flow of images that populate her world. It is for this reason that we must oppose the trigger warning—not because we want the right to show any and all materials whenever we want but because it gives rise to an understanding of self that makes us vulnerable to paternalistic modes of protection. (541)

In contradistinction to this view, we see trigger warnings as a recognition of students' active engagement in class. Faculty members regularly ask students to come to class prepared, and that means completing the reading before class, bringing needed materials, and the like. As instructors, we frequently tell our students what to expect in the reading. For instance, before students read theoretically dense work, we might say: "The reading for Wednesday is probably the most challenging piece we will read all semester. Give yourself some extra time with it, and take notes about places where you get lost or have questions. The beginning, where the author explains the theory she uses, is much harder than the rest—so if you feel overwhelmed, keep going, as it does get easier as you go along." This statement is not a trigger warning, but an example of a routine way to equip students with extra information that helps them prepare most effectively for class. Does using this statement in class make us complicit in "paternalistic modes of protection"? Or does it make the class discussion more robust and energizing because students made it to the end of the reading without giving up on page four because they feared they were alone in not understanding high theory?

Assuming that such a statement does not inspire the polemics of a trigger warning, why is a similar statement, one that accounts for trauma, so controversial? For instance:

> The reading for Monday focuses on sexual assault and includes some graphic descriptions of legal cases of rape and intimate partner violence, so I want you to realize that and be prepared for it. As we discuss the reading on Monday, remember that we expect people to be free to share openly and agree or disagree civilly (with the reading, with the instructor, or with each other). Please be aware that this is a common enough experience that we likely have students in class who have experienced it (or know someone who has). Feel free to do what you need to do during that conversation to take care of yourself.

In our view, offering students either of these statements, the content preview or the trigger warning, recognizes students as active agents involved in their education, not the defenseless wimps Halberstam imagines and maligns. Neither warning excuses students from the readings because of their denseness or potentially triggering content, but both recognize that students who are fully prepared for class will have a better experience completing the reading and discussing it. Moreover, both statements acknowledge that students may need to leave class discussion for any number of reasons (using the restroom, needing to breathe, or feeling sick—rare indeed is the faculty member who expects an ill student to vomit in the classroom). More importantly, both treat students not as objects on whom instructors impose readings, lessons, and assignments (and whom instructors discipline if students do not engage in normative ways), but instead as subjects who make their own decisions about how best to engage with the material, including how best to participate in class conversations. In other words, from a framework of consent, trigger warnings invite students to engage authentically in ways that respect their intellectual, emotional, and bodily dignity and autonomy.

Crafting classrooms that invite students to wrestle with difficult material, including explicit permission to disagree civilly (without
engaging in hate speech or character attacks), has profoundly enriched
our own experiences as teachers. For example, in an online conflict communication class that includes readings about intimate partner violence,
we have observed that letting students know ahead of time about the
content has allowed them to feel empowered and more willing to share
their own experiences. The lecture video students watched included a
preview of the topics to come as well as a brief introduction to the concepts in the articles. The video explained that one reason people might
remain in abusive relationships is that abusive partners sometimes create material conditions in which care for the couple's children depends
on the abusive partner's income. While no requirement exists for students to self-disclose, one student's discussion-board post noted that in
her abusive relationship, she left *because* she had kids—and as such, she
disagreed with the point in the lecture. This comment inspired a smart
discussion of the different options available to people in abusive situations depending on various contingent circumstances. While we cannot make an empirical conclusion from this anecdote, we believe that
the preview of the potentially triggering material facilitated the student's
willingness not only to share her experience but also to do it in a way that
openly contradicted the lecture video.

### Creating More Just and Livable Campuses

We have focused so far on trigger warnings in classrooms, but we
agree with Jeremiah Hickey's (2016) observation that a concern about
potentially triggering material goes beyond classrooms on any given
university campus. When the University of Wisconsin–Milwaukee
allowed Milo Yiannopoulos to project photographs of a transgender
student, misgender her, and threaten to rape her, the student in question felt that she had no choice but to leave the university. She and
other students had protested Yiannopoulos's invitation, but the university—in the same spirit as Ellison's commitment at the University of
Chicago—allowed Yiannopoulos to speak under the guise of freedom
of speech (Overpass Light Brigade 2016). The university's chancellor, Mark Mone, wrote a letter to the campus community afterward,

emphasizing that he disagreed with Yiannopoulos but valued freedom of speech (including, apparently, freedom of hate speech) and "opportunities to hear diverse viewpoints" (Mone 2016). He also insisted that the university must remain welcoming to lesbian, gay, bisexual, and transgender students, and shockingly, "I also will not stand silently by when a member of our campus community is personally and wrongly attacked." What Mone misses in his response is the uncomfortable reality that the two values he upholds in this case in fact conflict. Despite Yiannopoulos's history of hate speech, Mone did indeed "stand silently by" when students asked the university to intervene in Yiannopoulos's invitation.

The situation in Milwaukee may seem extreme, but Mone is not the only free speech advocate whose adulation for unrestrained expression knows no limits, up to and beyond material harm. In her consideration of trigger warnings, Goldberg (2016) expresses concern that universities may apply laws against sexual harassment too rigorously: "laws against harassment at universities and the workplace . . . may restrict too much protected free speech, if the bar for when sexist and racist speech rises to the level of harassment becomes lower and lower" (742–43). In other words, should we allow *some* sexist and racist speech as a way of ensuring we do not become too restrictive?[4] Kate Manne and Jason Stanley (Manne and Stanley 2015; Stanley 2016) have argued that conservative students' claims to marginalization on campus constitute part of a "free speech fallacy" that "weaponizes" free speech as propaganda: "The notion of freedom of speech is being co-opted by dominant social groups, distorted to serve their interests, and used to silence those who are oppressed and marginalized. All too often, when people depict others as threats to freedom of speech, what they really mean is, 'Quiet!'" (Manne and Stanley 2015). In other words, weaponized free speech is wielded to protect the powerful, silence the marginalized, and maintain the status quo. When marginalized students (and faculty) protest or critique those higher up in the social and institutional hierarchy, they are often read as exhibiting "insubordination, defiance, or insolence. When things go the other way, it tends to read as business as usual" (Manne and Stanley 2015).

Yiannopoulos's threatening language may be acceptable to some, but the student he targeted at UW–Milwaukee wrote a scathing response to Mone in her letter of withdrawal from the university, demonstrating the fear and harm she experienced:

> What I did not anticipate was being specifically targeted and called out in the way he did. I hadn't said anything or made even the slightest disruption: He had his harassment of me planned out well in advance. I'm sitting there and I hear him say "(my name)" and I just froze up. I have never, ever, ever been more terrified in my life of being outed. Ever. He put my picture up, which as already stated, was taken from a prior period when my masculine features were significantly more sharp and extremely noticeable. And I am sitting there frozen in total terror that somebody around me would recognize me, point me out, and incite the mob of the room against me. Nobody did point me out, thank god. But do you have ANY idea how much power Milo had and how it feels to pray that your ability to "pass" doesn't fail you now? That's what it was like. (Overpass Light Brigade 2016)

The student's response brings the tension between the university's two stated goals—welcoming trans students and allowing free expression—into sharp relief. Like many university administrators, the chancellor wants to believe he can have both, but when the two come into conflict, he privileges free expression—even violent, harassing expression he would have been within his legal rights to stop—over the trans student's safety and wellbeing. This, we believe, is an oddly fundamentalist (as well as privileged) view of freedom of speech. Boyer's (2002) essay on academic freedom enclosed with the University of Chicago letter extols the "virtues of intellectual openness and fearlessness," but Boyer refers to fear from reprisal for expressing disparate beliefs (95). Perversely, Boyer ignores the fear and material harm hate speech does in the lives and bodies of those targeted.

By contrast, we call for campuses of consent in which student dignity and autonomy are a central means of cultivating critical engagement and critical thought. By "campuses of consent," we do not mean that students always choose or dictate course readings, content, and discussion as well as campus speakers (a primary fallacy held by many in the anti–trigger warning camp). Instead, we mean campuses that prioritize access and engagement and that proactively work to center lived student experiences in order to cultivate not just their minds but also their bodies and spirits. We view consent as a fundamental pedagogical issue, including a range of practices of which trigger warnings are only one part (see chapter 5). On a campus that respects the dignity and autonomy of all students, those with histories of trauma or a need for accommodations cannot be dismissed or infantilized as "fragile" or in need of "coddling" or "protection." Instead, we recognize mental health and wellbeing, as well as dis/abilities, as realities that—like their physical counterparts—have material effects on students' education. Moreover, we view requests for help in any form as the opposite of weak—indeed as strong, assertive, proactive, and engaged. This is especially true for marginalized and historically disadvantaged students, who must articulate their needs more often to faculty and staff who are unaware of how best to help. For this reason, our commitment to trigger warnings reflects the social justice values that undergird our approach to teaching. As Zúñiga (2013) argues, social justice "values critical consciousness, participation, connection, passion, bridge building across divides through dialogue and action, and alliances and coalitions for change as pathways to individual and collective empowerment, equity, safety, and security for all social groups" (590). Furthermore, our proactive view would also account for students who are unable or unwilling to ask for help directly (such as students with undiagnosed disabilities, students who cannot afford to obtain a medical diagnosis, or students whose needs fall outside a medical-centered disability model).

We view the ideal of a socially just campus as necessary, if not always fully possible. The privilege to feel safe, valued, and able to speak one's mind is not equally available to all, even on the most progressive campuses. Belief and doubt (not to mention respect) attach unequally to students (and faculty) with or without race, gender, cisgender, ability, neurotypical, and class privileges. But we argue that precisely because students without these privileges are so often marginalized, instructors have the opportunity and obligation to model a different dynamic in the classroom, one that aims at the highest ideal of inclusiveness and conversational equity. While instructors cannot control every factor in the classroom that might contribute to such an ideal, we can think consciously about how we might proactively foster (and model) socially just conversations.

In order to understand better what students are and are not asking for when they request trigger warnings, we have reframed the debate in this chapter by asking *what can trigger warnings do?* We might also ask *what does an anti–trigger warning stance do?* We argue that trigger warnings invite consent from students and investment in their own education, while an explicitly anti–trigger warning stance (such as the one taken by the University of Chicago) reflects assumptions that are fundamentally anti–student-centered, skeptical of the realities of mental illness and disabilities, and invested in a neoliberal model of personal responsibility and individualist grit ("get over it") that characterizes much of the contemporary cultural and political moment. Focusing on the rhetorical and material effects of trigger warnings allows us to respect students' boundaries and make higher education more accessible. It also allows us to redefine what universities mean by "free speech" and "academic freedom." Even beyond the university, "free speech" is not equivalent to each individual's right to say whatever they want. Free speech is always constrained by laws and customs, and it is never absolute. In any given society, the speech of the powerful and privileged always has major advantages over the speech of marginalized groups, who may be forbidden or discouraged to testify in legal settings or who may be dismissed, ridiculed, or discredited when they do speak. Democracy is presumed to protect each individual's right to speech, but feminists and critical race theorists have long shown that the public square is primarily a space for powerful White, straight men with property and wealth, in which others gain access to public debate at great risk to their mental and physical wellbeing, if at all (Berlant 1997; Gilmore 2017; Warner 2000). Consider, for example, the multiple death and rape threats Anita Sarkeesian faced when she posted videos on her website, *Feminist Frequency*, that provided a gender-based critique of popular video games with overused tropes such as the damsel in distress (Sarkeesian and Cross 2015).

If we acknowledge that speech is always contested, fraught, entangled in issues of power and visibility, and never purely "free," how does our view of free speech on campus change? We need to contextualize free speech rather than seeing it as an absolute guarantee. Such a view of free speech and academic freedom would allow us to take into account the concerns of students and faculty about hate speech and harassment, rather than dismissing these concerns out of a misguided fidelity to "free speech" or including "all sides" of an issue that is discussed on campus (Patterson 2016). Complicating the concept of free speech on campus would force us to reckon with the rhetorical situation in which any given speech act happens, which includes not only the rhetor but also the audience, cultural and historical contexts, and intertextual references. Finally, it would ask us to recognize the different privileges and oppressions that attach to different students, faculty, and invited speakers.

Moreover, if we view this question in the context of trigger warnings and consent—as we are suggesting here—how might our conception of free speech on campus need to adapt? In many ways, the ideal of "free speech" relies on the same fantasy of the Cartesian mind divorced from the body that many anti–trigger warning thinkers privilege. By contrast, campuses of consent as we envision them aim to be radically inclusive and to center the bodyminds of students. And although we reject the fantasy of purely "safe spaces" inaccurately defined as protection from difficult or controversial ideas, we propose that our model of pedagogical consent and radical inclusiveness supports teachers in creating classrooms in which students (as well as faculty) are free to make mistakes without judgment or shame and then learn from constructive feedback to do better next time (Spencer 2015a).

Trigger warnings, of course, are just one way of cultivating campuses of consent. But we believe that when defined and used effectively, they serve the important function of acknowledging and respecting students' physical, intellectual, and emotional boundaries. In our conception, trigger warnings are radically inclusive, holistic, prostudent, and downright pedagogically effective. Indeed, we might end with a further turn of the theoretical screw and ask: to what extent do arguments *against* trigger warnings function to coddle overly sensitive *faculty* who cannot bear to take suggestions from students about how best to teach them?

## CHAPTER 5

# SURVIVOR-CENTERED PEDAGOGY

## CONSENTFUL CLASSROOMS AND EPISTEMIC JUSTICE

A s we have shown throughout this book, while slightly more than 11 percent of college students of all genders (and 23.1 percent of undergraduate women) identify as survivors of sexual violence,[1] university campuses are often institutional spaces of nonconsent, both in the way they address (or fail to address) sexual violence and rape culture on campus and in the way they replicate the inequities and oppressions that make violence possible. But universities can also be(come) foundational spaces in which students learn about consent and sexual violence, as well as other forms of inequality and oppression, analytically and in depth. Even students who are not survivors, we submit, benefit from survivor-centered pedagogy, as well as from a wider institutional commitment to fostering campuses of consent that recognizes violence as systemic and structural, where the hierarchies of power that make survivors' bodies injurable and dismissable are not replicated. Faculty who care about social change (or simply about students) therefore have a tangible opportunity to examine how classrooms can become spaces in which violence—whether physical, emotional, or intellectual—is not dismissed but is instead meaningfully examined, theorized, and actively resisted.

Such a pedagogy is particularly imperative, we believe, at the current cultural moment because individualist narratives of personal responsibility that position students as consumers have proliferated in higher education over the last two decades, particularly at administrative and structural levels. The neoliberal university, which we have critiqued throughout this book, increasingly sees education as a way to groom employees for the global marketplace rather than as a public good (Wagner, Kulbaga, and Cohen 2017). As Penny Jane Burke (2014) argues,

> neoliberalism increasingly restricts our pedagogical imagination, concealing the ways that educational encounters form subjectivities, ways of being and doing. However, neoliberalism works in complex ways with other oppressive forces, such as patriarchy and institutional racism, to limit our conceptualization of "diversity" and "difference." (391)

At many institutions, "diversity" and "inclusion" are buzzwords intended to illustrate the value and relevance of tokenized difference in the world economy (Burke 2014, 390; see also, Ahmed 2012; Spencer and Patterson 2017). Intellectual labor is rebranded in the "knowledge economy," and education becomes about the production of commodified knowledge and skills for profit (Bissonnette and Laval 2017, 6). The neoliberal university constructs students in nakedly capitalist terms as nascent corporate subjects, their eventual employability relentlessly prioritized over other aspects of their personhood, and "professionalization" becomes a primary pedagogical goal even in many undergraduate humanities departments. Students sometimes internalize this discourse, seeing themselves as consumers purchasing valuable degrees and "investing" in their future careers by securing huge amounts of loan debt from for-profit banks. And as faculty, staff, and students are stretched thin in the absence of adequate state funding, universities encourage increasing levels of bodily discipline and emotional stoicism to keep us productive. In this environment, any kind of education that does not contribute to the growth of global capitalism and its values is viewed with suspicion if not disdain.

What does any of that have to do with consent? Higher education in the United States has long been invested in replicating the gendered, racialized, and classed hierarchies of the culture at large. The neoliberal university adds to the proliferation of hierarchies a rhetoric of individual self-interest and competition (often couched dangerously in the pseudo-feminist language of "empowerment") that obscures how structural discrimination and violence work, both at the university and in the larger culture. It also constructs a set of institutional norms and policies that equate knowledge production with profit and success with social compliance (as when marginalized students critical of powerful speakers or campus policies are silenced, a phenomenon we discuss in detail in the previous chapter). These rhetorics, norms, and policies have become widely dispersed throughout the university, including in classrooms. Is it any wonder, in this context, that students are quick to blame themselves if they experience violence or if they cannot mold themselves into diligent "bodyminds" (Carter 2015) for the global workforce? Here, we see the truly insidious nature of the meritocracy myth: for someone to make a profit, someone else must take a loss—but mathematical realities get eclipsed by bootstraps narratives that, under neoliberal logic, put all agency and responsibility squarely on the shoulders of individuals. (We might instead recognize the role of state funding cuts for higher education and predatory lending practices on the part of banks.) When they graduate with debt into an economy that offers them precarious wages, properly neoliberal students blame their own lack of initiative and effort rather than these structural forces.

Neoliberalism, we are suggesting, begets, and then excuses, violence. Moreover, if violence, as we argue here, is a tool of oppression, then faculty need to do more than simply teach *about* violence and consent. We need to *enact* nonviolence and consent in our classrooms and in our teaching practices, in part by critiquing neoliberal policies and discourses on our own campuses (as we do in this book). Enacting consent as pedagogy requires us to reconsider the ways in which epistemically privileged discourses and hermeneutics, as well as hierarchical teaching practices, function in higher education to perpetuate power and violence in the world. In the words of G Patterson (2016), we must "model a way of considering the worldmaking power of discourse and its ability to render us (un)human" (145).

Drawing on our commitment to critical feminist pedagogy as well as the philosophical concept of "epistemic (in)justice" developed by Miranda Fricker (2009) and others (Allen 1996; Chafetz 1997; Harding 1991; O'Brien Hallstein 1999; Pohlhaus Jr. 2011; Wood 1995), we argue that a survivor-centered pedagogy is rooted in consent as radical respect for students' physical, intellectual, and emotional boundaries. Such a pedagogy is not solely about teaching content; it also works to decenter toxic, hegemonic White masculinity and its privileged ways of knowing. Instead, the epistemics and experiences of women, students of color, queer students, trans students, students with disabilities, and working-class students are actively foregrounded. A survivor-centered pedagogy, we argue, validates students' personal experiences, identities, and narratives, while respecting students' various ways of learning (for example, without solely privileging speaking up in class). It values nondominant identities, narratives, experiences, and ways of knowing as authoritative and expert, and positions reflective institutional critique as central to teaching and learning. Finally, it exposes and reflects on neoliberal ideology and discourse, including within the university, and works actively to reframe violence as a structural tool of oppression and a communal, not personal, responsibility. Each of these features of survivor-centered pedagogy, we argue, goes a long way toward cultivating consentful classrooms.

While much of the critical pedagogy literature emphasizes a student-centered classroom that attends to all students' voices in class conversation by privileging dialogue (Freire 1970; hooks 1994; O'Reilley 1993), we suggest that speaking up in class is not always possible for all students (or necessary for their learning); moreover, requiring students to speak can even be problematically normative, colonizing, and masculinist. Not all students are able to participate in that way (for example, some survivors, nonnative English speakers, or students with certain learning disabilities), and instructors and classmates are sometimes not ready or willing to hear their perspectives. Furthermore, listening, thinking, and other quiet learning skills are just as crucial to participatory learning. This is one way in which a pedagogy that considers survivors' needs and boundaries is helpful for all students.[2]

In other words, we advocate listening for and respecting student consent: just as we would not force someone to press charges or to testify in court, we ought to respect a student's decision or need not to participate vocally. Especially as "coming to voice," a concept originating in consciousness-raising movements and women of color feminisms, is co-opted by neoliberal (popular) feminism and the self-help industry (Berlant 2008; Brown 2013; Duggan 2003; Gill 2016; Gilmore 2010; Grewal 2005; Kulbaga 2008, 2016; Lakämper 2017; McRobbie 2004; Neville 2012), we can be reasonably skeptical of how it sometimes becomes privileged in student-centered teaching (and at the expense or loss of what?). But we attend not just to speaking: as Leigh Gilmore (2017) and Kate Manne (2018) have shown, cultivating supportive, empathetic listening (witnessing) is also crucial, since judgment and doubt attach disproportionately to women when they speak about violence, and empathy attaches disproportionately to perpetrators in what Manne calls "himpathy" (197).[3] The classroom is a space where power and privilege coexist with oppression and legacies of harm and violence. Survivor-centered pedagogy fosters a range of ways to engage with the material and values diverse ways of knowing.

## KNOWLEDGE IS (EPISTEMIC) POWER

Our argument builds on the work of women of color feminisms and critical feminist pedagogy in the Freirian tradition (Brown 2009; Davis 1983; Freire 1970; hooks 1994; Lorde 1984; O'Reilly 1993), as well as new work in feminist epistemology (Fricker 2009; Pohlhaus Jr. 2014) and in feminist theories of witnessing (Gilmore 2017) and misogyny (Manne 2018). Much of the earliest work in critical pedagogy importantly theorizes teaching as having the power to oppress and/or liberate. In *Teaching to Transgress*, for example, bell hooks (1994) examines "the difference between education as a practice of freedom and education that merely strives to reinforce domination" (4), arguing that the U.S. education system cloaks itself in a veneer of "objectivity" and "facts" but works in service of White supremacy, capitalism, and patriarchy. This is teaching as a tool of oppression. hooks argues that "education as a practice of freedom" requires new theories rooted in the personal experiences and stories of women students and students of color. She writes:

> I came to theory desperate, wanting to comprehend—to grasp what was happening around and within me. Most importantly, I wanted to make the hurt go away. I saw in theory then a location for healing. When our lived experience of theorizing is fundamentally linked to processes of self-recovery, of collective liberation, no gap exists between theory and practice. Indeed, what such experience makes more evident is the bond between the two—that ultimately reciprocal process wherein one enables the other. (59)

For hooks, experience is "a way of knowing that coexists in a nonhierarchical way with other ways of knowing" (84), and a key goal of transgressive pedagogy is to invoke personal experience, including the experience of the material body, as authoritative, not "merely" subjective, and certainly not beside the point.

But experience is also constructed through ideology and other forms of power and oppression (Scott 2001), and when students reflect on it, or speak about it, they are entering an unequal epistemic scene. Recent work in feminist philosophy on epistemic injustice (Fricker 2009; LeBlanc and Kinsella 2016; Pohlhaus Jr. 2014) suggests the extent to which justice is a matter of testimonial competence (being equipped to hear and understand stories of harm and violence) (Dotson 2011, 242–44). Although hooks was writing over a decade before Miranda Fricker (2009) developed the theory of "epistemic injustice" to name how someone can be wronged specifically in their capacity as a knower, that is the kind of harm hooks alludes to when she points out that personal experience is often discredited as a way of knowing. Fricker specifically explores two kinds of epistemic injustice: *testimonial injustice* and *hermeneutical injustice*. She explains:

> Testimonial injustice occurs when prejudice causes a hearer to give a deflated level of credibility to a speaker's word; hermeneutical injustice occurs at a prior stage, when a gap in

collective interpretive resources puts someone at an unfair dis-
advantage when it comes to making sense of their social experiences. An example of the first might be that the police do not
believe you because you are black; an example of the second
might be that you suffer sexual harassment in a culture that
still lacks that critical concept. We might say that testimonial
injustice is caused by prejudice in the economy of credibility;
and that hermeneutical injustice is caused by structural prejudice in the economy of collective hermeneutical resources. (1)

Both forms of epistemic injustice can occur in classrooms. For example,
a teacher or classmate may not believe a student who shares an experience of discrimination, or a class activity or lecture may be structured
in an ableist way, but students may lack the language to name it as
ableist. In our view, epistemic injustice is a form of violence that makes
other forms of violence possible (as in the sexual harassment example
quoted above). Cultivating classrooms of consent is a way of fostering
epistemic justice, and by extension social justice.

This becomes especially important when taking into account the
violence and trauma that affect students' lives. As we argued in chapter
4, though students' personal responses and life stories are often dismissed in dominant pedagogy paradigms as feminized, "merely emotional," or a form of uncritical thinking, we believe that students' life
stories, bodily experiences, and emotions ought to be valued in a consentful classroom. But more than this, we need to attend to the ways
in which experience is gendered, raced, and classed and storytelling by
women and people of color is automatically judged, doubted, silenced,
and/or shamed (Gilmore 2017). Because violence and oppression are
normalized in our ways of knowing about the world, they are themselves epistemically privileged (for example, when elementary school
American history students learn that though George Washington held
slaves, he freed them upon his death, they are invited to recognize him
as magnanimous—and the violence of slavery gets a pass; similarly,
when sexual violence is taught as a "women's issue," it is subtly coded
as not men's problem).

Feminist educators may know that many students, statistically speaking, have experienced violence of various kinds, including emotional and epistemic violence, but they may still be surprised to learn how trauma affects student learning. Wagner and Magnusson (2005), writing specifically about sexual violence, have shown that past assault or abuse poses "a legitimate barrier to learning" (449). This is at least partly due to the ways in which survivors' experiences, knowledges, and needs are ignored and erased by an educational system that alienates them at best and pathologizes them at worst. Sexual assault and abuse are institutionalized and culturally sanctioned forms of violence, rather than rare or aberrant (454). Urging feminist teachers not to construct survivors as deficient or limit them to a single aspect of their identities, Wagner and Magnusson suggest instead that we open up academic discourse to other ways of knowing:

> [Academia's] unwritten rules are rigidly enforced even within women's studies classrooms, as faculty feel compelled to operate within these institutional parameters of the inflexible university. This message may be conveyed subtly, in the way that professors guide classroom discussions, or it may be more blatant, as in the case of a teacher who immediately refers a woman who has disclosed violence to an outside support system, averting further engagement with her. In this way, women are further fragmented and the message is reinforced that such complexities of women's lives are not considered appropriate topics for discussion within the academic setting. (457–458)

In other words, these "unwritten rules" can constitute a form of epistemic injustice. Moreover, we would add that even in the case of *written* rules, such as new university policies (in response to Title IX and Clery Act requirements) that classify faculty and staff as mandatory reporters, survivors are harmed by the presumption that *others* know best whom to tell and how to offer support. Erasing survivors' autonomy in this way is a further epistemic injury in an already tangled maze of legal and bureaucratic harms facing a college student who discloses violence.

Burke (2015) likewise examines how the lived experiences and emotional lives of women are devalued or commodified in the neoliberal context of higher education. She argues that academic spaces disregard emotion, and therefore come to fear difference since emotions attach to those who are differently gendered, raced, and classed. This is the case despite the nominal embrace of corporatized notions of "diversity" used in marketing the neoliberal university (391). Certain "bodies are pathologized through misogynistic discourses that manipulate fear of the 'feminization of higher education.' Characteristics associated with difference in [higher education], such as 'being emotional' or 'caring,' are regulated and controlled through a range of disciplinary technologies. . . . Difference and emotion are posed as dangerous forces that require homogenizing and neutralizing via technologies of managerialism and through the fixing of socially constructed categories (388, 390)." In the classroom, Burke shows, fear of difference is often projected onto students perceived as Other through dominant discourse and the practice of shaming, which can be vocal or not (395). Neoliberalism then reframes student shame as lack of individual self-esteem addressable by student services offices. Thus "students from 'Other' backgrounds are often characterized . . . through a range of deficit disorders, including lack of confidence" (397).

We explored Leigh Gilmore's (2017) theory of the "tainted witness" in depth in the introduction, but we note here that what Gilmore describes—the ubiquitous, institutionalized disbelief of women and people of color, including survivors, when they speak about their lives—is a similar form of epistemic violence. And it is one that has been exacerbated by neoliberalism. As Gilmore puts it:

> Victim blaming obscures the context surrounding any specific person; it is consistent with a neoliberal distortion of responsibility. . . . Seeing victimization as cooperation or participation asks of women, what did you do to deserve this? And, in so doing, falsely represents women's vulnerability to harm as their culpability and recasts the compromised situations in which they live (relationships, workplaces, homes of various kinds) as willful choices or even risky behavior. (10)

Put another way, "doubting women is enshrined in the law, represented in literature, repeated in culture, embedded in institutions, and associated with benefits like rationality and objectivity" (19–20). Gilmore does not address higher education specifically, but classrooms are crucial spaces in which "judgment disproportionately affects the vulnerable" (13) and "objectivity [aligns] against the dispossessed" (15).

How, then, do we create consentful classrooms? We find Megan Boler's (1999) theory of a "pedagogy of discomfort" convincing, one that resists the numbness of what she calls "passive empathy," a recognition of others' suffering that "produces no action towards justice" (161). This is an uncomfortable pedagogy because it requires students (as well as teachers) to examine and analyze our responses to knowing about suffering or trauma, and to acknowledge the limits of our knowing rather than taking refuge in immediate certainty or platitudes about the chronological inevitability of progress (such as "it gets better"). Importantly, a pedagogy of discomfort means not that faculty intentionally set out to make students uncomfortable; instead, it recognizes that the classroom can never become an always-comfortable space, nor will learning always comfort. Instead of displacing the emotional and sticking only to "facts" or abstract theories, Boler locates learning in self-reflection, the questioning process, and the self's relation to others: "learning to live with ambiguity, discomfort, and uncertainty," she writes, "is a worthy educational ideal" (198). Indeed, many students already live with ambiguity and discomfort in their daily lives, and giving room to explore the positive potential of not-knowing fosters students' intellectual and emotional consent (again, not comfort or complacency) by removing the imperative to know the answer or to "master" a subject intellectually and without emotion. Asking better questions—rather than seeking definite answers—is a key goal of feminist pedagogy, and to ask better questions, students need to feel safe enough to disagree respectfully with their instructor and other students (Spencer 2015a). But crucially, *safety* here does not mean the kind of "safe space" so commonly criticized on Fox News or by anti-trigger warning academics. Instead, it means the classroom must be a place where students may make mistakes and welcome correction or conversation (not judgment and rejection) from their instructor, classmates, or both.

Likewise, in constructing a survivor-centered pedagogy, we do not advocate for instructors to take a so-called neutral view, especially given that the kind of pedagogical "objectivity" known as "neutrality" (and often encouraged by the neoliberal university) works in service of epistemic injustice. As G Patterson (2016) argues,

> While multiply minoritized teachers have sometimes adopted pedagogical neutrality as a matter of survival, this does not give the rest of us an alibi. Too many of us have moved through educational spaces with unchecked epistemic privilege and have adopted neutrality as an extension of genuine goodwill toward our students without questioning how appeals to the student-as-everyman consolidate racial, sexual, gender, cis-gender, and religious oppression in the classroom. (145)

If we then reject both a one-size-fits-all classroom politic that insists on its own way (we do!) and a pedagogical neutrality that gives structural oppression a pass (we do!), what kinds of classrooms do we advocate? We suggest that consentful classrooms begin to answer this question (or, perhaps more properly, guide us to ask better questions).

## THE CONSENTFUL CLASSROOM

As teachers, we may have a good amount of epistemic privilege, though if we are marked as women, people of color, immigrants, disabled or crip, queer, or trans, that privilege is complicated by lived experiences of oppression. We believe that these lived experiences can be mobilized in service of a more just classroom, what we call a *consentful classroom*. A consentful classroom is one in which students are invited to participate willingly and actively in knowledge production and meaning making in ways that work for them and that celebrate their contributions. In a consentful classroom, teachers are mindful of students' learning needs, including needs that are not accounted for in mainstream pedagogical theory, and we are also respectful of student boundaries, even if they are indirectly communicated. If, for example, a student identifies as dyslexic and exhibits extreme distress when asked to read aloud, we ought to recognize and respect that boundary and seek out other ways she may participate. Likewise, if a student shares a personal experience with the class or teacher, she should be able to expect her story to be believed, validated, thoughtfully responded to, and kept confidential. In other words, the consentful classroom is one that is survivor-centered, attendant to the experiences of anyone who has been harmed by violence and oppression.

A consentful classroom is not, however, a space without joy or creative play. Rather, in the spirit of Ruth Nicole Brown's (2009) "hip-hop pedagogy," we believe that *actively celebrating* the presence and thinking of non-White, women, queer, and trans students is part of our work, especially since these identities and experiences are often excluded altogether from education. As Brown puts it, "Recognizing the intellect, humanity, and daily negotiations Black females make, regardless of age, under less than inspiring constraints underscores a political project of Black girlhood celebration" (20).

In the remainder of this chapter, we reflect on what, specifically, a survivor-centered pedagogy entails and offer some practical examples. We show how a consentful classroom acknowledges individuals' perspectives and epistemologies, affirms diversity in learning style as well as identity, includes self-reflexive and institutional critique as significant in the learning process, and works to reveal and undermine the operation of neoliberalism.

## Validates Personal Experiences, Identities, and Ways of Knowing

As we describe in the previous section, a key component of the consentful classroom is validating students' personal experiences, identities, and ways of knowing. This is particularly important for survivors, women, students of color, and queer or trans students, whose experiences are often dismissed or ridiculed in dominant discourse or whose identities and ways of knowing are simply erased. Some students, of course, resist learning about certain forms of difference (Johnson, Rich, and Cargile 2008; Spencer 2015a). In response, faculty must actively, consistently contest epistemic violence and acknowledge and validate alternatives (we might call them *counter-epistemics*) in order to ensure that hierarchies do not simply repeat or morph in form but not content.

An example from disability studies may prove instructive. In *Body Horror*, Anne Elizabeth Moore (2017) offers a compelling account of what such erasure of identity is like. Moore describes becoming disabled but not identifying as "disabled" or "crip" for eighteen months after her diagnosis, despite being familiar with disability studies from her academic work. She concludes that her lag in identifying as crip could be explained by the lack of cultural representation of crip lives and language:

> What I wish to point out is that the historical erasure of crips, as reflected in the recent dormancy of that word itself, contributed directly to my inability to describe my lived experience to others. In fact, the communication struggle became another barrier, an additional impairment. The historical erasure of crips is an emergent cause of disability. (168)

Moore goes on to write about how her specific bundle of disabilities (autoimmune disorders) have only very recently been accepted as genuine by the medical establishment, and even today these disorders are difficult for people to get correctly diagnosed. Perhaps unsurprisingly, the majority of autoimmune sufferers are women (75 percent according to Moore), and because the symptoms (pain, nausea) are invisible, even knowledgeable doctors have a habit of dismissing them as psychological or exaggerated. In other words, the experience of autoimmunity is one of being consistently doubted or disbelieved. According to Moore, one function of writers—and here we would add teachers—is to make language available for describing experience, especially experiences of pain and oppression:

> One way to elucidate the failure of a dominant system is through language: crafting vocabulary to identify the constituent elements of a shoddy structure, articulating points of weakness or inflexibility. . . . For language to function as

communication, however, all parties must share vocabulary, must be open to new words and meanings, and must generate the patience required to adapt to them. . . . The word crip proves this is not assured; the word crip proves that, in fact, the disinterest in certain particular forms of difference is very resilient indeed. (170–71)

Building on Moore's insights, we might say that experiences of epistemic harm (such as the testimonial injustice she describes when dealing with doctors and publishers and the erasure of meaningful language for her identity and experience) create barriers that accrue to existent oppressions (such as being a woman and a person with a disability). Notably, identifying as "crip," for Moore, is an intensely personal and embodied process; it is not merely academic. Taking the term to heart requires time, reflection, and a painful realization that many will not "be open to new words and meanings" or have "the patience required to adapt to them" (170).

What is instructive about Moore's experience is that, as teachers, one of our roles is to model and mentor the process of being open and patient enough to allow students to wrestle (often painfully, slowly, and nonlinearly) with new concepts and unfamiliar language. The kind of ambiguity and uncertainty that Moore describes having with the word *crip* reminds us that identity is felt and personal, not solely theoretical.

Students' names and pronouns serve as one clear example. While it ought to be obvious that students have the right to choose the identifications and other descriptors we use to communicate with them in class, it is by no means common pedagogical practice for teachers to ask students for their pronouns, respect that their names may not match what the official roster says, or honor the identities they embrace as their own without tokenizing them. For trans students in particular, the first day of class when the instructor calls roll can easily turn into an episode of epistemic violence, including misgendering, deadnaming, and potentially outing someone to the class. Although some students attempt to preempt such embarrassment by emailing the instructor before class begins, relying on student initiative in order not to be outed reveals the violence of cisnormativity. Faculty concerned with creating consentful classrooms may find more creative ways of calling roll, such as asking students to introduce themselves or just calling last names from the roster and letting students announce the name they use (an accommodation that also makes sure students who use a nickname or their middle name get addressed properly throughout the term).[4]

Beyond names and identities, we also value and acknowledge students' experiences. In many classrooms, it is still common to dismiss personal experience as a way of knowing (by, for example, forbidding students to use "I" in academic writing or subtly guiding class discussions past uncomfortable personal moments). For many academics who have internalized a narrow view of learning, the personal is indulgent, narcissistic, or simply irrelevant, something students use to derail discussion when they have not done the reading. We think it is reasonable for teachers and students to expect learning to consist of *more* than personal storytelling, of course, but many students engage the learning process with their memories, bodies, and hearts as well as their minds.

In a creative nonfiction writing class, for example, one of our students (here called Michaela) shared a beautiful narrative about her experience of homelessness as a teenager. Michaela's story was full of details such as the drug overdose of a friend and two different scenes of sexual violence, one of being groped on a bus and the other of a rape in a friend's car. It was also full of heartwarming moments of extraordinary friendship and community building between teens and adults at one shelter in a downtown Midwestern metropolis. In no small part because of the story's poetic language and humor, it was clear that Michaela, who was now in her second year as a nursing student, wanted to bring this story to life without cultivating pity or contempt in readers for her younger self or her community of friends and acquaintances of all ages who experienced homelessness. Michaela chose to workshop the story with the entire class. Because large-group writing workshops can sometimes be unwieldy, resulting in an overabundance of advice for the writer, students provided letters to the writer in which they identified at least one strength of the piece and at least one suggestion for revision. In their letters to Michaela, several students noted how much they had learned from her story and how it had helped them to reflect on assumptions they routinely make about people who experience homelessness, use drugs, or run away from home as teenagers. While the large-group discussion focused on helping Michaela to make cuts, all students who were present that day urged her to keep the complexity of her portrayal—the tragic and violent as well as the heartwarming—intact. For Michaela, the workshop was a powerful affirmation of her strengths as a writer as well as her identity and experiences, and the students' celebration of her story brought her to tears and briefly made her consider switching majors and becoming a creative writer. (Michaela graduated from the nursing program two years later and continues to write creative nonfiction.) This was a student who may have expected her interlocutors to respond with disbelief, judgment, shame, or blame, but instead was affirmed and offered constructive writing feedback in addition to nonjudgmental support. She learned from her classmates, and they learned from her, the importance of witnessing experience, in Gilmore's (2017) words, "without deforming it by doubt, and without substituting different terms of value for the ones offered by the witness herself" (5).

### Respects Various Ways of Learning

In a consentful classroom, teaching must be flexible and responsive to a given group of students, the class dynamic, and the sociopolitical context. As we argue in chapter 4, radical accessibility is a key component of intellectual consent, and it must be conceptualized beyond a medical model that pathologizes particular ways of learning and privileges others. Instead, faculty should use Universal Design for Learning (UDL) principles, which encourage multiple means of representation (texts), action (assignments), and engagement (motivation) (National Center on Universal Design for Learning 2015). While UDL is often viewed as a way of accommodating students with disabilities, it is in fact good pedagogical practice for all students.

Beyond UDL principles, the consentful classroom is one in which students have an intellectual and emotional stake in learning because their interests, ideas, and identities are valued as meaningful. And not just in the abstract—they are centered in the work of the course. Respecting various ways of learning, in practical terms, means fostering as many opportunities for students to participate in meaning-making as possible. Faculty might, for example, provide opportunities for students to discuss a given text in large- and small-group discussion, individual written reflection, and online discussion boards. Such a model allows for the learning styles of students who prefer to work with others, would rather work alone, or enjoy learning online. It does not rely solely on spoken contributions to discussion, which may not always be possible for all students, but it does make students' words and thoughts central "texts" of the course.

In her work with veterans in a war literature course at a two-year community college, Mary O'Reilley (1993) finds that she often has to make space—actively and consciously—for emotions of all kinds, her own and her students'. For O'Reilley (1998), who writes eloquently about the spiritual work of teaching, "to teach is to create a space . . . These are revolutionary words, because most of us think in terms of filling a space: filling the number of minutes between the beginning and end of class, filling the student's notebook, filling the student's head" (1–2). Instead, she urges faculty to cultivate spaces in which nothing much at all appears to be happening (such as time for thinking, reviewing a reading, or writing in a private journal), but in which all manner of thinking, feeling, and learning can take place. For her students, a space to reflect on the trauma of war and the grief they carry is a space of learning.

We often have to work harder, both intellectually and emotionally, to respect students' various ways of learning. We must set aside some of our academic training, which has inculcated us with a fairly limited idea of intelligence and success. But the results can be very creative. For example, in an Introduction to Women's, Gender, & Sexuality Studies (WGS) class, students have a choice of final projects: they can write a traditional research paper on a course topic, design a community workshop or high school course, or create something visual, audible, and/or textual that demonstrates what they learned through research. Some students write brilliant research papers of the traditional variety, and other students have composed a syllabus and lesson plan on gender identity for high schoolers, performed a flash mob about teen dating violence at the local high school, put together an annotated music playlist about body positivity, performed spoken word, written and performed original music, shared personal narratives from their lives, written and illustrated a children's book that was published and printed for their child for Christmas, and designed instructive board games and video games that are playable by class members. In their course feedback, students report that these creative or activist projects are more challenging than traditional assignments, but nonetheless they are excited about coursework for the first time. Students report that they learn more from doing these nontraditional assignments as well because they are so personally invested in the work and because it taps into a wholly different learning style from what they are used to.

### Positions Institutional Critique as Central to Teaching and Learning

In a consentful classroom, one of the most meaningful ways of destabilizing cultural norms and hierarchies is to reflect deliberately and actively on the teacher's and students' own campus and classrooms. We teach regularly about our institution's policies, programs, and language regarding sexual violence, making some of the same critiques we make throughout this book. Inviting students to participate in institutional critique enables them to think about issues discussed in class in "real-life" terms. It encourages them to make connections among classroom learning, academic research, and the various rhetorical spaces of campus. Sometimes, it results in student activism that continues outside the classroom and has a lasting effect on campus culture.

At our institution, we have had regular opportunities to address how sexism, racism, classism, homophobia, transphobia, and sexual violence on campus are handled by various actors and offices. For example, in fall 2012 in a co-ed dormitory on campus, a student posted a flyer titled "Top Ten Ways to Get Away with Rape." Administration did not immediately notify students about the flyer until a student, who was also vice president of the student organization Women Against Violence and Sexual Assault, posted a picture of the flyer on

Twitter. The story gained national media attention, after which a faculty forum was held to address rape culture on campus. That semester, in Introduction to WGS, we spent class time reflecting on the language of the flyer, the concept of rape culture, the prevalence of sexual assault at our university and on campuses around the country, and the slow and inadequate response of administration. Two students (10 percent of the class that term) went on to complete final projects on the topic, one a cogently argued research paper titled "Top Ten Ways to Prevent Rape on Campus" and the other a plan for a community workshop on rape culture, with speakers and a brochure featuring local statistics and resources.

We can learn a good deal from our students in the process of reflecting on campus culture. They give us a sense of the gender politics of the living spaces on campus, the social norms at sorority and fraternity events, the culture of alcohol and drug consumption, and their views on university crime alerts.[5] In 2012, we had more than one heated discussion about whether the "Top Ten" flyer could be construed as a joke, and if so, whether—and in what rhetorical contexts, and to whom—rape jokes can be funny. We often spend more class time focused on institutional critique than we expect to because students bring up relevant examples regularly. Of course, they have various opinions about how best to address violence on campus and about the administration's actions.

## Exposes and Critiques Neoliberal Ideology

More often than not, institutional critique dovetails with critiques of neoliberalism.[6] A consentful classroom is one that exposes and critiques neoliberal ideology and discourse, offering students language for describing what it is and providing alternatives to the cultural tyranny of personal responsibility, positive thinking, and self-help. Given how neoliberalism commodifies identity and reifies narratives of overcoming adversity through hard work on the self, it is especially important that students learn how structures and systems contribute to individual choices, available opportunities, and life trajectories.

In the context we examine in this book (twenty-first-century U.S. higher education), neoliberalism does more than encourage students to internalize self-help discourse. It constructs students and faculty in moralized terms as "good" or "bad" university subjects in a system that rewards overwork and discourages thoughtful critique and powerful feeling. To the extent that universities invite students and faculty to think about sexual assault, for example, neoliberalism (along with consumer laws such as Clery) frames the conversation as a matter of personal student vigilance and ostensibly "responsible" or "irresponsible" decisions (drinking/not drinking, going out alone/practicing the buddy system) rather than as a common and specifically oppressive form of violence rooted in privilege, entitlement, and power. Individual perpetrators are framed as aberrant and possibly devastated by the charge of rape, and cases are slowed so that accused students may finish out the athletic season (Guest Pryal 2015). Victim blaming, already "consistent with a neoliberal distortion of responsibility" (Gilmore 2017, 10), takes new forms that extend outward from the crime into its aftermath, as counseling services and student "success" programs encourage survivors to embark on a journey of self-healing. At one major public university, a student's therapy records were seized from student counseling services by administration and handed over to the university's general counsel to help defend against her lawsuit: "They [used] her own post-rape therapy records against her" (Guest Pryal 2015), citing the Family Educational Rights and Privacy Act to do so. While this is not a common occurrence, it does caution us that corporatized universities may prioritize reputation, public relations, and defending against real or potential lawsuits over student wellbeing.

The neoliberal narrative of the survivor who overcomes the violence she experiences and emerges stronger (like other narratives of overcoming adversity) is familiar to students from music, television, film, video games, and literature. In the world of such narratives, trauma is construed as a kind of sacred birth, from which a new self finds joy and purpose. The cultural contexts that enable violence are not examined, nor is social change considered as a remedy. Instead, the survivor learns (or simply knows) that healing is an individual journey, and redemption an individual achievement, difficult but holy. Or, in fictional representations such as those found in *Buffy the Vampire Slayer* and *Sweet/Vicious*, individual survivors team up for a presumably empowering and feminist form of vigilante justice.[7] Such narratives can be comforting, perhaps, because they seem to offer agency, justice, and healing. But the agency at issue is focused on individuals rather than community and culture. As Sarah Deer (2015) suggests, frameworks of justice that individualize violence and healing do little to address rape as a community wrong requiring communal responses. Students need, then, to examine neoliberal discourse both at the university and in culturally available narratives about sexual violence. And they need alternative models such as Deer's and alternative narratives that put pressure on the master narrative of individual trauma and healing.[8] Otherwise, students who struggle to heal, decline to forgive their attackers, have trouble getting on with their lives, falter in maintaining their grades, or reject sacralized wholeness-journey metaphors are at risk of feeling like healing failures, while social structures and institutions remain unexamined.

We find that our students enter introductory WGS courses open to the idea that gender discrimination exists, that feminism is necessary, and that women's rights are human rights in the abstract; but often their theoretical and rhetorical frameworks for understanding those key terms—gender discrimination, feminism, human rights, even women—are neoliberal and market-based, constructing capitalism and the power of the free market as able to empower individual women and even to rectify human rights violations, such as pay inequity, discrimination, and violence. Moreover, and perhaps unsurprisingly, we find that their frameworks are limited by singular definitions of "women" and "feminism" that sometimes buckle when we examine how power and oppression operate differently in, say, Iceland or Bangladesh, or when we consider queer- and trans-based feminisms that look different from the neoliberal rhetorics of women's "empowerment" promised in mainstream media culture.

Because our classes are diverse in terms of race, ethnicity, and socioeconomic class—over 40 percent of our students are Pell-grant-eligible, about 20 percent are non-White, and about 30 percent are first-generation and/or nontraditional—many of our WGS students occupy social locations at odds with dominant neoliberal rhetorics of meritocracy and free choice. At the same time, however, they are sometimes invested in the neoliberal promise of empowerment through free markets, consumer purchasing power, and self-help. We find a transnational and rhetorical feminist approach to be helpful in offering counterdiscourses to this promise. Strategically layered readings and assignments get students thinking rhetorically about the key concepts of WGS as a discipline—gender, feminisms, human rights, social justice, and the marketplace. The advantage of a rhetorical approach to these key gender-studies concepts is that it works against "fixing" any term in a single, static definition. Instead, we examine the contextuality (and *rhetoricity*) of the concepts, including their persuasive purpose in a given text, their embeddedness in larger cultural discourses, and the importance of audience. While students sometimes want fixed terms they can apply in any context, our classrooms actively resist such universality even as we demand a counterdiscourse to neoliberalism and its rhetoric of disembodiment.

In Introduction to WGS, students read a variety of nonfiction narratives of sexual assault from the United States, including excerpts from transgender activist Janet Mock's *Redefining Realness: My Path to Womanhood, Identity, Love and So Much More* (2014) and narratives from non-U.S. women, specifically in contexts of imperialist aggression or war, including Shailja Patel's *Migritude* (2010). Initially upon encountering rape in literature for the first time, students respond with a combination of outrage and pity in written reflections and in class discussion (what Boler [1999] calls "passive empathy" [161]). They tend to cast survivors as abject and powerless, perpetrators as evil, and the problem of sexual violence as an inexplicable, individualized injustice with no clear solution (or as explainable through evolutionary psychology and its gender-regressive politics such as "boys will be boys"). Sometimes they engage in the rhetoric of American exceptionalism, offering as a panacea the thought that we are lucky to live here, where rape as political warfare (described in *Migritude*) supposedly never happens. However, those initial assessments fail to hold up when we discuss the rhetorical situation of these narratives. Both Mock and Patel illustrate how violence thrives as a tool of oppression. In Mock's memoir, the neoliberal narrative of the individual journey (or "path") is reclaimed in service of educating readers about injustice for Black trans women. The scene of her assault exposes the logic of antitrans violence, which is presumed to be deserved because she is believed to be disguising her "true" identity on a date with a cisgender man. We discuss this scene in detail, articulating the cruel logic of the deserving victim in the wider context of antitrans violence (especially against Black trans women) in the United States. In the memoir, it is very clear that rape is a tool of transphobia and racism. Likewise, in Patel's (2010) narrative, rape is a weapon of war and colonialism in the British labor camps in Kenya during the Mau-Mau uprising (1952–1960). In a chapter titled "The Sky Has Not Changed Colour," Patel draws on multiple women's oral testimonies in order to voice this silenced history of rape warfare by British soldiers, a collective gendered, racialized, and colonialist history dismissed and buried by British media interests. The section concludes succinctly: "International tribunals have confirmed that rape is a form of torture" (47).[9]

The word "torture" requires us to reassess dominant U.S. narratives of rape as an individualized crime. Similarly, Mock's sendup of the concept of "deserved" violence for Black trans women asks us to reconsider how rape is justified, normalized, and thereby perpetuated. Each author invites readers to locate the origin of violence in oppression, and thus to recognize that structural change is the only reasonable remedy. After writing initial responses to the texts, the class breaks into small groups tasked with thinking about how each author forecloses an emotional response of passive pity and what the author is calling for instead—such as understanding, belief, and commitment to social change.

## CONCLUSION: DANCING WITH JUSTICE

Throughout this chapter, we have theorized the consentful classroom, one that centers survivors' experiences, critiques rape culture on campus, respects students' intellectual and emotional boundaries, and positively affirms human dignity—including validating students' various abilities and identities. While we have focused on creative writing and WGS classes in our examples, the principles of survivor-centered pedagogy and the consentful classroom apply across the disciplines.[10]

Ramzi Fawaz's (2016) metaphorical understanding of classrooms as dance floors resonates with what we envision:

> The dance-floor and the classroom are strikingly similar. Both are spaces people frequent on a weekly basis where they meet a mixture of strangers, friends, and acquaintances to engage in acts of intimacy: the flow of bodies and exchange of ideas. Like dance floors, classrooms demand the formation of stranger intimacies, where we come to know, take seriously, and engage directly with other people, face to face. We lock eyes with others and something unfolds from that look that is often beyond our capacity to predict. Both spaces have the capacity to transform how we relate to and flow with other people; and just as any good DJ curates a musical selection to orchestrate the mood of a dance floor, so too an instructor is tasked with shaping the emotional atmosphere of a class to draw students in and encourage them to 'dance' with one another. We are also tragically aware that classrooms and dance floors are spaces whose social energy and utopian potential can be snuffed out by violence—we have become nearly as accustomed to seeing guns enter these spaces as energetic bodies, ideas, and exchanges. Yet more than anything, classrooms and dance floors can be spaces that incite countless pleasures: the pleasure of shared ideas and bodily sensations, the pleasure of expanding one's network of relations, the pleasure of losing oneself in a collective practice, only to find oneself again reborn at the end of a session or long night of celebration, more attuned to others. These pleasures are not theoretical or abstract, but *experiential*. To participate in a classroom is as grounded, and worldly of an act as dancing in a club, and both models [*sic*] numerous ways of being with others in public space. (139)

We embrace Fawaz's vision of the dance-floor classroom and extend his metaphor only slightly, to include consent more explicitly (certainly he nods toward it)—especially because we know dance floors also offer predators cover to violate others' physical space. Just as consensual touch, carefully timed and coordinated between dancing partners gives a dance its beauty and artfulness—and makes the experience enjoyable for all dancers—a consentful classroom requires respect and intentionality to choreograph the best possible educational experience for students and faculty alike. Such a classroom fosters epistemic justice, the dance of various ways of knowing, and therefore contributes to a just world on campus and beyond. And the dance becomes a just way of knowing, learning, living, moving, and being in the world: a world of radical consent.

---

# CULTIVATING CAMPUSES OF CONSENT

As we were completing this project, the *New York Times* reviewed two books that argued against the necessity of reconceptualizing consent on college campuses, *Unwanted Advances: Sexual Paranoia Comes to Campus* (Kipnis 2017) and *The Campus Rape Frenzy: The Attack on Due Process at America's Universities* (Johnson and Taylor 2017). In *Unwanted Advances*, Laura Kipnis argues (foreshadowing Betsy DeVos) that Title IX officers on campus have far too much power and that the current generation of feminists has abandoned empowerment and embraced victim status. Drawing on her experience as the target of a Title IX investigation on her campus, Kipnis invokes several hyperboles, writing that Title IX cases are as bad as "McCarthyism" (1) and the "Inquisition" (22) and constitute a witch hunt tantamount to those of seventeenth-century Salem (passim). The university campus has become a "penal colony" (37) comparable to the "Saudi legal system" (87) where "gold digger[s]" (85) can accuse professors and other students of sexual assault capriciously and Title IX officers with revenge fantasies against men can get "payback" (134). Throughout the book, Kipnis conflates sex and sexual assault, nostalgic for the days when sex between faculty and students was considered prosaic; she denies inherent power differentials based on social and institutional roles.[1] Kipnis offers this solution to a potential sexual assault situation: "Why couldn't Catherine say no to going on the date from the start? Why would she go to the apartment of a guy she already didn't trust? This isn't victim blaming. It's grown-up feminism" (218–19). Kipnis identifies herself as a leftist feminist several times in the book, but what does feminism mean to her when she suggests that women drink alcohol in order not to have to worry about consent ("you hear, in case after case, about women drinking so much they're incapable of saying *yes* or *no*. It doesn't seem unreasonable to ask if one of the benefits of blackout drinking is not having to decide" [197])?

The other book in the *New York Times* review, K. C. Johnson and Stuart Taylor Jr's *The Campus Rape Frenzy*, is perhaps more troubling, although unlike Kipnis, Johnson and Taylor make no attempt to paint themselves with a feminist brush. As the title and subtitle suggest, the authors argue that "extremists on campus" have manufactured a crisis that inflates statistics and misrepresents faculty, staff, students, and administrators as uncaring and indifferent to sexual assault. These vaguely identified extremists have invented this crisis, Johnson and Taylor suggest, in order to compel universities "to presume the guilt of accused students"—leading to the "attack on due process" identified in the subtitle. In this unfair system of adjudication, "accused students effectively have to prove their innocence, often under procedures that deny them any meaningful opportunity to do so" (2).

In the world imagined by *The Campus Rape Frenzy*, women college students eagerly participate in "casual hookups" (2) that they later regret. Young men accused of rape are very often the "victims" (2) of uncredible accusers. The policies at colleges and universities, especially those advanced by President Obama in 2011 (which we discuss in chapter 1) are presumably stacked high in favor of accusers and against the accused. For example, this typical passage from the book describes "how most colleges handle sexual assault allegations these days" (8):

> Start with an alcohol-soaked set of facts that no state's criminal law would consider sexual assault. Add an incomplete 'investigation,' unfair procedures, and a disciplinary panel uninterested in evidence of innocence. Stir in a de facto presumption of guilt based on misguided Obama administration dictates, ideological zeal, and fear of bad publicity. It's a formula for judging innocent male students to be sex offenders. (8)

Drawing on a small number of anecdotal examples of cases in which an accuser allegedly falsely reported a rape or retracted a statement,[2] Johnson and Taylor insist that what "extremists" call "rape culture" actually springs from "a patronizing view of women—portraying them as weak or ignorant, incapable of making their own choices" (68). According to this view, strong and smart women students are apparently not raped because they are capable of making their own choices and choose not to be victimized. In their retellings of the anecdotes, which are narrated with high drama and a palpable hatred for women who report rape, Johnson and Taylor repeatedly emphasize excessive drinking as well as a lack of "physical or medical evidence to corroborate" (174) rape, ignoring the fact that such evidence is in reality not common.

Like Kipnis, Johnson and Taylor enjoy historical comparisons, and they suggest parallels between the current "campus rape frenzy" and both the internment of Japanese Americans during World War II and the Salem witch trials (12). Perhaps most tellingly, they relate it to "efforts to punish free expression of views that [extremists] mischaracterize as sexual (or racial) harassment" (12). In other words, the book is critical of progressive policies related to gender and race *in general*, among them the pursuit of justice for survivors of sexual assault. The authors are therefore especially interested in demonstrating the innocence of college athletes accused of sexual assault. In their view, athletes sometimes receive special treatment but are more often victimized by "incredible" (172) accusers. *The Campus Rape Frenzy* ends by suggesting that in order to ameliorate the danger men students face of false allegations on campus, parents should investigate "the ideological and pedagogical diversity among faculties"—a clear sign that the authors believe that universities are indoctrinating students in liberal ideology and that conservative faculty, who are more likely to excuse or deny sexual assault on campus, provide a tempering force in an otherwise maniacal search for more men to accuse falsely. Unsurprisingly, it also asks parents to urge their children not to use alcohol, a classic victim-blaming prevention tip; on the other hand, surprisingly, or perhaps cheekily, it recommends that young men in college either practice celibacy or videotape all sexual encounters—"including foreplay!" (269)—to avoid false rape accusations. Taylor and Johnson's basic ideology is captured in this single sentence, imaginatively directed at a nonexistent son about to go off to college: "just as women in college face grave dangers from rapists, . . . men like you face grave dangers from false accusers and—even more—from other young women who have been misled by colleges and activists" (268).

Both books deserve long and eviscerating reviews, as we suspect they will receive in other contexts. We describe them here to underscore not only our point that consent on campus desperately matters, but that cultivating consent is a radical act, one under increasing attack from the right and left. And while both progressives and conservatives claim to care about the "crisis" of sexual assault on campus, when changes to the legal or social structures that underpin higher education are suggested, it becomes clear that people actually care about a specifically narrow, normatively gendered, racialized, and classed young woman, whose presumed "purity" has been soiled.

We are deeply concerned about the backlash against feminist gains that has characterized U.S. culture more generally since the rights movements of the 1960s and 1970s, the forty-fifth presidential administration being only the most recent iteration. Education Secretary Betsy DeVos's announcement in September 2017 that universities are no longer required to follow a "preponderance of the evidence" standard in adjudicating suspected cases of sexual assault, and can now use a much more difficult to prove "clear and convincing evidence" standard, was accompanied by familiar arguments about how the futures of accused young men are ruined by overzealous Title IX staff, feminist faculty, and regretful or revengeful women students (U.S. Department of Education 2017). What unites these regressive critiques, we believe, is the investment in neoliberal discourses and policies, including breezy constructions of "women's empowerment" and an ethic of personal responsibility and constraint that seems to attach only to women. Through this attachment, women are "responsibilized" by neoliberalism; as Gilmore (2017) puts it,

> when young women are told to watch their own drinks at
> parties, to designate someone to watch out if another woman

disappears from a party, and to wear or not to wear particular clothing in order to avoid rape, "responsibilize" describes the anonymous voice that deceptively labels ready-made blame as helpful advice. (12)

If higher education is to take effective action in response to sexual assault, harassment, hate speech, or any of the other violent consequences of inequity and oppression, it must extract itself from the grip of neoliberal ideology and begin to think about injustice as a shared community responsibility.

Throughout this book, we offer a number of critiques of conventional wisdom about consent, learned and scholarly conclusions about consent, legal treatments of consent, and common campus practices around consent—including those at our own university. We see the principle contributions of this book as threefold. First, we present an expanded understanding of consent that recognizes the importance of intellectual and emotional boundaries in addition to physical ones—and acknowledges that these are always interrelated. Second, we illustrate the value of the close criticism of what Zarefsky (2004) calls "the uniqueness of exemplary cases" as well as "recurrent patterns" with a goal to "seek insight and appreciative understanding" (607). We look to our campus not to make generalizable conclusions about all campuses (though our conclusions no doubt apply to many) but to reveal how campus cultures create and sustain contexts of violent nonconsent. The kinds of meaning our analysis reveals transcend questions of statistical significance by instead pointing to cultural practices and policies that harm and that can and ought to be improved. Third, we embrace an approach to cultural studies critique that not only interrogates the problematic, but also envisions better futures. Even as we resist a narrative that requires pat happy endings or tidy conclusions, we offer (in this conclusion and throughout the book) practical suggestions to effect change at the individual and structural levels.

Sharp critiques come with risk because they challenge the practices and even worldviews of the status quo, including in higher education. Our critique began with our own university and extended as our research unfortunately revealed that the patterns we noticed resonate with university and college campuses around the United States. We have never heard anyone use the word "coy" to describe either of us, and the critiques of our campus we undertake in this book we have done openly and often loudly. We began this project out of a shared desire for a campus less steeped in rape culture; more reflective of the ways it produces, protects, and even exacerbates toxic masculinity; more supportive of survivors and other marginalized students; and, ultimately, more centrally concerned with prioritizing radical consent. Our felt need to work toward cocreating more livable and just campuses resulted in this book, which has been accompanied by varying levels of support and pushback at our university.

Of course, we recognize our privilege in being able to levy critiques against higher education in general and our own institution in particular.[3] We realize that staff or faculty in contingent positions (especially part-time) may need to exercise more caution than we do, if they have the opportunity to make these sorts of critiques at all. And while the neoliberal university understands students as customers-who-are-always-right, we recognize that some students reading this book who support our argument will not have access to the contexts of power that can influence institutional decisions. Despite our privilege, however, we are aware too that our power is limited. As Sara Ahmed (2016) argues, it is exceedingly difficult to realize that at your own institution and throughout higher education, *the system is working* to enable violence and harassment. Like us, Ahmed recognizes that universities are institutions with cultures explicitly designed to allow for harassment and abuse, especially of marginalized faculty, staff, and students. She writes, "to work as a feminist means trying to transform the organizations that employ us—or house us"; however, "you can change policies without changing anything. You can change policies in order not to change anything." Ahmed's resignation from Goldsmiths, University of London was the direct result of this realization.[4]

Much ink has been spilled critiquing the neoliberal university.[5] We align with related critiques of missed opportunities to unmask structural and systemic oppressions in favor of individualized, personal solutions to complex problems (Dow 2001; Patterson and Spencer 2017). As we stated in the introduction, to enact our radical concept of consent in

practice at all levels of institutional and social life would require nothing less than the dismantling of what bell hooks (2000) calls the White
supremacist capitalist patriarchy, and with it rape culture, toxic masculinity, transphobia, heterosexism, and other interlocking oppressions.
We recognize these forces of oppression as systemic and structural, and
therefore resistant to change, but that does not mean we accept them
as inevitable or impenetrable. Gerda Lerner's (1986) observation that
patriarchy's constructedness implies its destructibility inspires us here;
throughout this book, we have shown how consent and its opposite (violence) are constructed, portrayed, resisted, enhanced, or diminished by
everyday policies, actions, messages, and behaviors on university campuses. All of these norms mean that other possibilities exist:[6] other ways
of constructing or deconstructing, portraying or rejecting, resisting or
supporting, enhancing or diminishing exist, and in uncovering those,
we can begin to live into them. In this way, our definition of consent is
*performative*—by doing it, we make it so. We write with hope but not
naivety—none of us alone can untangle a skein wound and twisted over
millennia, but we offer here ways to get started. To collaborate. To con-
spire. To enact consent, radically and productively understood.

Enacting consent on campus is the subject of the remainder of
this concluding chapter. We offer concrete suggestions about incor-
porating consent into university pedagogy, policy, and everyday interactions (which we call *microaffections* and *microsubversions*, echoing
work on microaggressions). We then wrap up with a final statement,
following Sara Ahmed (2010), about affirming the work of feminist
killjoys and rejecting the imperative of too-happy endings. These suggestions build on the practical strategies we have offered throughout
the book alongside our analytical claims.

## PEDAGOGY

Universities have many opportunities to educate students about consent: from orientation and welcome sessions to outreach to student
groups to the coursework students take in their majors and general
education requirements to the announcements sent about crimes
on campus. We support the thoughtful and careful use of all these

contexts as chances to emphasize the importance of consent and to define it more broadly and richly than in the conventional way, as we have throughout this book.

As chapter 2 contends, consent education works best (and reflects, in our view, the most radical politics) when it occurs consistently across time, not in isolated blotches, and in conversation with others rather than in solitude. Therefore, we advocate for a college curriculum that includes consent as a central narrative. We have suggested throughout this book that universities marshal the expertise of their faculty—particularly faculty in women's, gender, and sexuality studies and those in cognate areas with relevant research interests and credentials—in educating students, other faculty, and staff about consent. We do not mean that already overburdened faculty should take on more work. Rather, we can easily imagine how consent education can become part of a faculty member's typical load, when, for instance, consent becomes part of the required curriculum within particular courses, majors, the general education core, or interdisciplinary initiatives. Integrating this content into women's, gender, and sexuality studies courses is easy enough, but even in classes like conflict communication or creative nonfiction, we have found ways to address the role of consent in interpersonal relationships and autobiographical writing. We imagine most other humanities and social science classes can feature or perhaps even center conversations about consent, including emotional and intellectual consent as we have theorized them here. Even math courses could make use of statistics about violence as an opportunity to open informed conversation about consent. Where possible, lessons about consent work best when they center the voices of those multiply minoritized.

By creating classes about consent or even just including a single relevant reading, lecture, or activity, we encourage our faculty colleagues to invite students into a process of institutional critique as part of learning about consent. As we argue in chapter 5, we see value in revealing rather than concealing not only institutional practices themselves, but also the politics of those practices, to our students. Pragmatically, asking students to critique the politics of their own institutions often has the effect of engaging their interest more than a hypothetical case study or a remotely located "true story." But more than that, engaging in institutional critique reveals the topic's relevance to students and even mobilizes them to action. For example, one of us worked with students who wanted to stage a counter-demonstration to a student group's anti-choice display (a lawn full of white crosses) on our quad. Our students recognized the links between class content and the display outside the window, and they took action, creating a corresponding (and much more brightly colored) lawn full of inclusive, accurate information about reproductive justice. In fact, that action has had a longstanding effect on our campus. Each spring, a new group of women's, gender, and sexuality studies students constructs a reproductive justice display, and we now have a student organization dedicated to gender equity and reproductive justice. We have also used university policies and announcements in our classes to illustrate how power functions within organizations to surveil or discipline bodies and behaviors and constrain employee consent (e.g., the "premium discount option" on our health insurance plan that involves giving our employer access to our medical records and even a sample of our blood!). We believe in institutional critique beyond issues related to consent, but the questions of consent we raise throughout this book have a place in many classes. Chapter 1 critiques our university's crime alerts, and analyzing those alerts in class has generated some of the most robust discussions in our courses. The alerts show students that the politics of victim blaming apply not only to their individual friends and classmates but also to institutions.

We also urge extending the pedagogical and scholarly conversation about violence and consent beyond U.S. institutions to other contexts in the United States and around the world. Gender-based violence (including sexual violence) is the most widespread human rights abuse in the world, according to the United Nations Population Fund, affecting an estimated 35 percent of women worldwide (2017). Campuses should be places where students (and faculty) study rape as a weapon of war (and of so-called peacekeeping), the role of sexual assault in the prison-industrial complex, forced sterilization, and femicide, for example. We know that violence escalates during humanitarian crises, both because women's bodies are used intentionally to dominate and humiliate a geopolitical foe and because protection systems collapse during crises, leaving women and girls vulnerable. Transnational feminist scholars have analyzed how sexual violence thrives in imperialist spaces, including so-called peacekeeping missions in the Central African Republic, Haiti, and elsewhere (Deschamps, Jallow, and Sooka 2015; Harrington 2010; Higate 2007; Higate and Henry 2004; Kronsell and Svedberg 2012; Moncrief 2017; Nagel 2014; Odello and Burke 2016; Simi 2010; Skjelsbæk 2007). Because sexual violence is a key tactic used to oppress, it flourishes in imperialist and authoritarian spaces and where wealth is distributed unevenly. And while we focus in this book on the context of higher education in the United States, students benefit from understanding how discrimination, oppression, and inequality function to cultivate violence wherever they occur. Moreover, decentering the U.S. perspective allows us to understand how, as narratives circulate, belief and credibility attach to certain subjects and not others—to young, White, normatively gendered college women, for example, and not to Syrian refugees in Turkey. As Inderpal Grewal (2005) has suggested, public and scholarly discourse about sexual violence in the United States constructs young White women survivors as "deserving" subjects in a nationalist and neoliberal way. And as Wendy S. Hesford (2011) has convincingly shown, when such violence enters into representation and rhetoric, even in human rights campaigns, it risks (re)creating spectacle and perpetuating regressive nationalist and gendered norms. Therefore, it is imperative to attend carefully and critically to whose vulnerability and humanity are valued and whose are not.

Beyond encouraging discussions with students about institutional practices, we also see value in including students in consent education as peer educators. Not only do peer educators gain valuable skills in leadership and public speaking, but they also have a chance to connect with and relate to their peers in ways faculty cannot. We believe, following Grigoriadis (2017), that college students are often creative and savvy about negotiating consent in their own relationships and in challenging rape culture as they work to address sexual assault on campus. In many ways, students are expert in this area, and we ought not construe them as ignorant or naive but should instead help them to articulate what they already know from their daily lives and experiences. Peer education can also flatten power differentials that may make asking certain questions of a faculty member a challenge. And whether peers, faculty, staff, or teams that combine them offer consent education, we encourage presentations and visual aids (including memes!) that: define consent positively; categorically reject rape myths (the miscommunication model of sexual assault and the utmost resistance standard); construct consent inclusively for all genders and sexualities and in a sex-positive manner that does not contribute to paternalistic panic about protecting young women; and that conceptualize boundaries as intellectual and emotional, in addition to physical.

## POLICY

With respect to policy, we encourage university administrators, student services staff, residential advisors, faculty, and other stakeholders to see federal and state requirements as minimums and starting points. As we show in chapter 1, university staff appealed to state and federal laws to shut down our advice about better framing the language of crime alerts, but in fact, the law as written neither requires the harmful language our university used nor prevents the university from going beyond minimum requirements to include more useful language about incidents and prevention tips informed by a critical feminist perspective. Similarly, in training students about consent or forming policy about trigger warnings, universities need not (and ought not) stop where federal legislation leaves off. Instead, colleges and universities should marshal the expertise of their staff, faculty, and student leaders to develop trainings, policies, news alerts, pedagogies, and programs that take a thorough, intersectional, critical feminist, queer, and trans perspective on conceptualizing consent. Fostering campuses of consent depends not just on individuals, but on institutional commitments to fulfilling both educational and ethical obligations; to do so means meeting *and going beyond* legal requirements.

Furthermore, in crafting policies, we urge campuses to keep all students in mind. Policies and programming based in residence halls, for instance, may do fine work in serving students who live on campus, but they leave out students who live off campus or commute. To take another example, many universities exempt married students from residency requirements—but given that cisgender women who experience violence are often targeted by intimate partners, married students need this programming as much as their unmarried peers. At universities that include regional campuses, like ours, residence-hall-based programming reifies and exacerbates existing divisions and inequities. As we make clear in each of the previous chapters, we maintain that universities must center the experiences of multiply minoritized students in conversations about consent and resist homophobic, transphobic, and cisnormative framings of consent—and cisnormativity's usual invisibility is no excuse.

The content of policies and programs should be inclusive and comprehensive, by which we mean actively aware not only of the diversity of gender identities and sexual orientations, but of the nuanced implications for consent that various identities represent. For instance, an inclusive policy would avoid reference to specific body parts in defining rape and sexual assault. Ethical policies must avoid victim blaming and rape myths, overt or subtle, and should eschew stereotypes about gender, gender identity, and sexual orientation. Anyone may perpetrate or experience sexual assault, and policies should reflect that reality explicitly rather than in some ostensibly gender-blind vagueness that leaves some students wondering whether their experience counts, qualifies, or will be taken seriously.

Related to our concern for reflecting reality, universities must recognize that some drinking and substance use will occur, even with the best alcohol education. All too often, a focus on drinking slips quietly (or loudly) into the realm of victim blaming. Policies about sexual assault must not punish witnesses and victims for substance use, and crucially, policies must avoid conflating substance use with sexual assault or excusing sexual assault by blaming alcohol and drugs. If universities communicate to students that a substantial number of sexual assaults involve the use of alcohol or drugs, they ought also to include a clear disclaimer that that substance use does not remove the ethical imperative to obtain consent, and that persons who are substantially impaired may not, by most legal definitions, consent. Here, as elsewhere, we urge universities to embrace their ethical and pedagogical missions rather than leading with a concern for avoiding liability and stopping at the minimum threshold.

That same principle, prioritizing mission over liability, ought to govern decisions about how policies translate into educational programming. Bystander intervention education, for instance, should actively work to resist rape culture and all its entailments, including victim blaming, toxic masculinity, homophobia, and transphobia. Intersectional educational programming informed by feminist, queer, and trans research would show the interconnection of all forms of violence and oppression. Such programming, for instance, might offer a nuanced analysis of the relationship between White supremacy and rape culture by scrutinizing stereotypes of Black hypermasculine predation and White feminine victimage.

Despite high-quality educational programming and all best efforts of even the most conscientious campuses, some students will still commit and others still experience sexual assault. When sexual assault happens, we urge universities to compose crime alerts and other responses that describe perpetrators in active voice and offer advice that explicitly resists rape myths and victim blaming. We encourage radical belief for survivors who disclose violence. For perpetrators, we resist the popular sentiment that long, harsh, juridical punishments (especially prison sentences) are the sole path to justice. Certainly perpetrators should not remain on the same campuses as the people they have assaulted, but neither do we advocate for a response that relies on or further buttresses the violent hegemony of statist control and the criminal punishment system. Restorative justice measures, such as those advocated by Koss (Koss 2010; Koss, Bachar, and Hopkins 2003), may be appropriate, though we emphasize that they are only appropriate when the survivor initiates the request—confronting or forgiving one's attacker may constitute part of the path toward healing for some survivors but not others. Crucially, survivors must retain control and agency over their own involvement in pursuing any kind of case against their attackers or any sort of resolution. We categorically condemn systems that force survivors into conflict resolution conversations or other interventions (including mandatory reporting policies on campus) that amount to a loss of control and revictimization for a survivor.

Although most of our recommendations about policy relate to policies about sexual assault, we address consent more broadly in this book, and as such, we also return to trigger warnings in thinking about policy recommendations. Trigger warning policies like the one at the University of Chicago, which we discuss in chapter 4, tout freedom of speech and academic freedom while seeming to curtail faculty freedom to offer trigger warnings voluntarily. Moreover, policies against trigger warnings may threaten students' freedom of speech and right to accessibility in the classroom. We urge university disability offices, as well as interested faculty, students, and staff, to advocate for workshops and educational programming about trauma triggers and the importance of sensitivity to concerns related to trauma. We observe that trainings about military veterans who experience post-traumatic stress disorder already do some of this work, but this type of educational programming seems to get disassociated from classroom content warnings. We celebrate that campuses work to ensure equal access for students who have served in the military, including those with a history involving trauma, and we hope the same level of concern can extend to other students who have experienced trauma. Finally, more broadly, we encourage faculty to construe disability and accessibility in more expansive terms than those provided by disability services, which require a sometimes unattainable medical diagnosis in order to address student needs.

## MICROAFFECTIONS AND MICROSUBVERSIONS

While we have thus far reflected on pedagogical and policy-related strategies for enacting consent on campuses, we recognize that readers may need strategies for doing so on a more micro level. Microaggressions are small, everyday interactions that communicate some degree of disrespect or discrimination to marginalized people. Lucy Miller (2015) has noted that microaggressions "differ from traditional conceptions of racism and other forms of discrimination in that the conscious intent of the perpetrator may be difficult to determine, leaving the victim to question the accuracy of her or his perception" (133). We wonder, with respect to consent, what might be the opposite of microaggressions:

perhaps small, everyday acts that work to strengthen and expand consent in interpersonal relationships, social arrangements, and even university structures. Two possibilities include *microaffections* and *microsubversions*. A Google search reveals that these terms are not original to us, but for our purposes, we theorize microaffections as everyday actions that support and include others and microsubversions as everyday actions that resist or undermine rape culture, toxic masculinity, and other oppressive systems. Microaffections and microsubversions are not mutually exclusive and independent categories, but rather can be understood as overlapping and intersecting.

For instance, displaying an It's On Us sticker, magnet, or poster that includes contact information for campus-based and off-campus confidential resources for reporting sexual and interpersonal violence may serve as a microaffection for someone who wants to reach out for help but does not know where to look. At the same time, the It's On Us visual works as a microsubversion against rape culture because it names the problem of sexual and interpersonal violence and affirms that preventing and responding to such violence are community responsibilities. Though we critically analyze the It's On Us video, "One Thing" (2018), in the introduction to this book, we support the Obama-era White House Task Force to Prevent Sexual Assault and the resulting national movement that "asks everyone—students, community leaders, parents, organizations, and companies" to join the collective conversation and take action to create more just and liveable campuses (It's On Us 2018).

To offer another example, our university recently classified all faculty and staff as mandatory reporters for Title IX violations. (For a critique of this policy, see the introduction as well as Cahill 2018.) Knowing that we teach courses like conflict communication, gender studies, and creative nonfiction writing—where in the regular work of the class, students sometimes disclose interpersonal violence in their own lives—we include in our syllabi a disclaimer about our duty to report and information about confidential resources, should a student wish to disclose without reporting. (At our institution, this duty does not include violence disclosed in student work, but it does include violence disclosed after class or during office hours.) A sentence or two on a syllabus may function as a microaffection by offering useful information to students and a microsubversion by declaring at the beginning of a class that students' disclosures belong to them—and we prefer not to see students give up control of their stories by sharing something they never realized would create an obligation to report.

Women faculty, queer faculty, trans faculty, and faculty of color engage in microaffections when we model language and behavior that validates the experiences of marginalized people and responds to hateful language and behavior with constructive critique. We engage in microsubversions when we model language and behavior that speaks truth to power on campus and takes the worthwhile risk of cultural and institutional critique. A thoughtful invitation to a specific student to attend an event, participate in planning a program, or join a group may function as a microaffection, and consistently speaking up in campus meetings for more inclusive language and policy—whether related to sexual assault or another problem, and whether or not the speaking up results in an adequate response—can also be a microsubversion.

As these examples illustrate, the link between microaffections and microsubversions matters because we want to make clear that our conception of microaffections deals in worldmaking care and compassion, not a sappy and shallow platitude that "love is the answer" without acknowledging that the only love that matters is love that sweats, does work, gets something done. By the same token, microsubversions are not innately destructive; they respond to rape culture directly or by clever subterfuge. Together, microaffections and microsubversions join with the larger, structural strategies we have described in this book and others yet to be imagined—which we know reside in the creativity of our readers and coconspirators—to contribute to the project of worldmaking. The goal remains, as always, the construction of more just campuses, communities, and worlds—spaces more livable and amenable to the flourishing of the human spirit.

## A FINAL WORD FROM FEMINIST KILLJOYS

Throughout the two years we have worked on this book, we have occasionally faced accusations of lugubriosity. Even well-meaning friends and colleagues have wondered if our sharp critique is necessary and appropriate. Some assure us that "things are so much better now," but precisely which things, and compared to when, and by what standards we ought to measure "better," seem unclear. We want to make plain that we reject sugarcoated narratives of progress or the idea that the passage of time in and of itself implies improvement in material conditions and policies. Artificial notions of progress must not anesthetize us to forces that oppress, destroy, and kill.

As such, we join Sara Ahmed (2010) in embracing, claiming, and wearing with pride the sobriquet "feminist killjoy" (38). Of the imperative to put a happy spin on feminist critique, Ahmed writes convincingly:

> What concerns me is how much this affirmative turn actually depends on the very distinction between good and bad feelings that presumes that bad feelings are backward and conservative and good feelings are forward and progressive. Bad feelings are seen as orientated toward the past, as a kind of stubbornness that "stops" the subject from embracing the future. Good feelings are associated here with moving up and getting out. I would argue that it is the very assumption that good feelings are open and bad feelings are closed that allows historical forms of injustice to disappear. The demand that we be affirmative makes those histories disappear by reading them as a form of melancholia (as if you hold onto something that is already gone). These histories have not gone: we would be letting go of that which persists in the present. To let go would be to keep those histories present. (50)

We join Ahmed in refusing to efface histories of violence that persist into the present (and thereby enable their persistence). But we join her, too, in rejecting a present that cannot be more than it is. If "bad feelings," to use Ahmed's words, may inspire us to action, we relish stoking the fires of negative sentiment, critical outrage, and righteous indignation. We hope these bad feelings incite bold action, fearless leadership, and more careful analyses of what consent can become and how higher education might take up its obligation, responsibility, and opportunity to lead us all into more consent-centric futures.

# NOTES

## Introduction: What Can Consent Mean on Campus?

1.  It's On Us has since updated the pledge offered on their website, inviting visitors to "join the movement" and to "commit to helping create a culture of consent, bystander intervention and survivor support" (It's On Us 2018).

2.  For example, in September 2017, Education Secretary Betsy DeVos rescinded key Obama-era guidelines that required colleges to use a "preponderance of the evidence" standard of proof in adjudicating sexual assault cases. DeVos called that standard "discriminatory" against those accused of sexual assault, said the Obama policy had "gone too far," and encouraged colleges to use a much higher standard of evidence, a "clear and convincing evidence" standard, instead. The latter standard makes it more difficult for colleges to take disciplinary action against students accused of sexual assault. See Saul and Taylor (2017) and "Department of Education Issues New Interim Guidance on Campus Sexual Misconduct," a September 22, 2017, press release (U.S. Department of Education). For a further discussion of this change, see the conclusion.

3.  While the allegations against Harvey Weinstein popularized the #MeToo hashtag and renewed the movement in 2017, both the hashtag and the movement were created by Tarana Burke in 2006, a fact not always acknowledged by media accounts (Battaglia, Edley, and Newsome 2019). Similarly, Anita Hill gave public testimony before Congress about a Supreme Court nominee in 1991, twenty-seven years before Dr. Ford's testimony against Kavanaugh, but was often erased from the latter discussion. Women of color have often been at the forefront of antiviolence movements and very often have not been credited for that work (for example, in the work to fight White sexual violence against Black women in the bus boycotts of the 1950s and 1960s, which led to the civil rights movement). See McGuire (2010).

4.  Scholarship on BDSM culture (especially Bauer 2014) has reframed consent and violence—often tangled up in normative assumptions and biases—in useful ways. We do not include roleplay violence or roleplay coercion in our concept of sexual violence because it is consensual.

5.  For a convincing philosophical analysis of the limitations of mainstream

media representation of rape (and resistance), see Linda Martín Alcoff's (2018) *Rape and Resistance.*

6.  Students elect not to report for many different reasons, and choosing not to report should be honored as an agentic act. This is another objection we have to blanket mandatory reporting policies, which have increasingly been adopted by universities (see also, Harris 2017, 2019).

7.  See the National Center on Domestic and Sexual Violence (NCDSV)'s (2017) Power and Control Wheel for a common example.

8.  We build here on bell hooks's (2000) concept of the White supremacist capitalist patriarchy.

9.  Recent work has usefully expanded the concept of physical consent to include any form of "assumptive touch" (Troost 2008), such as hugs and kisses among friends and tickling children (Bluhm 2016; Lehr 2017; Weiss 2016). See also Anker and Feeley (2011) for an examination of consent and nonconsent in organ donation procurement.

10. This should include not just heteronormative relationships and sexual practices but knowledge and respect for queer, polyamorous, aromantic/asexual, and BDSM expressions. See especially Bauer (2014).

## Chapter 1: Just Response

1.  For compelling alternatives to punitive approaches to justice, see Mary Koss's (2010; Koss, Bachar, and Hopkins 2003) work on restorative justice in cases of sexual violence. Koss emphasizes that in order for restorative justice to be a viable alternative in such cases, the survivor must choose that course of action.

2.  Jeanne Clery Disclosure of Campus Security Policy and Campus Crime Statistics Act, 20 U.S.C. § 1902(f) (2012). The length of the full text of this law makes citations to it less than helpful. Readers who want to locate the relevant sections of the law can use the "find" feature electronically. The full text of the law appears online here: https://www.law.cornell.edu/uscode/text/20/1092.

3.  All fifty states passed Megan's Laws (which require sex offenders to register and community members to be notified of their names and addresses) during this period. Other states passed or considered additional shaming sanctions; in Ohio, for example, lawmakers proposed that registered sex offenders be required to use neon-green license plates. Residency restrictions and zoning laws restricted sex offenders' housing and employment upon release. Nearly half of states increased mandatory minimum sentences for rape. Such laws did not address the barriers for survivors of sexual violence in the criminal justice system, nor did these laws lead to an increase in convictions.

4.  See chapter 4 for a more thorough analysis of how the trigger warning debates dovetail with our interest in reconceptualizing consent on campus.

5.  Beverly McPhail (2016) has suggested that feminists ought to rethink the

power-and-control explanation for sexual assault, noting that offenders often list sexual gratification, revenge, or performance of masculinity as their motive. While we appreciate McPhail's critique, her reliance on self-assessments of motive from attackers misses the larger theoretical argument about the power dynamics within rape culture that work to legitimize these and other explanations for sexual assault. Moreover, the alternative motives McPhail lists are inextricably linked to power and control (as well as privilege). Finally, to understand sexual assault as a crime of power and control does not mean offering power and control as a monolithic explanation for attackers' self-professed motives. McPhail acknowledges that power and control can be a motive, a means, or an effect of sexual assault—yet she refutes the idea that power and control alone motivate rape. In other words, our concern about depoliticizing rape transcends the question of motive and speaks to means and effect as well.

6. Solnit (2016) makes a similar claim about the Centers for Disease Control's (CDC) new guidelines for drinking: "What is a woman? According to the CDC, all women are in danger of becoming pregnant. 'Drinking too much can have many risks for women,' their chart tells us . . . in a few deft, simple strokes [the CDC] reduces all women to fertile females in their breeding years who have what you might call exposure to fertile men. It denies the existence of many other kinds of women and the equal responsibility of at least one kind of man. Maybe it denies the existence of men, since women seem to get pregnant here as a consequence of consorting with booze, not boys." One might make the same claim of these suggestions to avoid drinking as a way of avoiding rape.

7. See Marine and Nicolazzo (2017).

8. Suzy D'Enbeau's (2017) study of a university sexual assault response team revealed marked differences between staff responses by occupation. She found that human resources staff and lawyers, focused primarily on compliance, did not mention advocacy or support for students when they talked about their roles on campus. Human resources professionals' lack of empathy for students often frustrated student affairs staff, who exhibited more compassion and care for students.

9. Because sexual violence violates and fragments the survivor's identity, many scholars have described rape as *spiritually* violent, in addition to physically and psychologically violent. Sarah Deer (2015), for example, argues that justice for Native survivors needs to be reimagined beyond legal and psychological remedies to establishing a "sovereignty of the soul" (xvi), and clarifies that "I use *soul* almost agnostically to refer to deep, fundamental aspects of identity. . . . In some languages, the more appropriate word might translate to *heart* or *spirit*" (xvi). See also Archard (2007), Card (1996), Henderson (1987), and West (1993), among others.

10. See chapter 3 for a fuller discussion of how consent is defined in online campaigns.
11. While we work as faculty and not in an advocacy role at our university, we collectively have over ten years of volunteer experience in hospital and court advocacy for survivors of sexual assault and intimate partner violence, and we have been teaching and researching about gender and gendered violence for over a decade. This, combined with our disciplinary expertise, leads us to believe that universities not only can better conform to required federal reporting laws while also better supporting survivors, but that they have a moral obligation to do so.
12. See Ann Cahill (2018) for a compelling case against blanket mandatory reporting requirements, which are not required by federal law but are increasingly being adopted by universities anxious to comply more easily with Obama-era Title IX expansions such as the "Dear Colleague Letter." Cahill (2018) writes, "the Obama-era guidances in no way required or even recommended such a blanket mandatory reporter policy; instead, the OCR [Office of Civil Rights] recommended consistently that each institution determine carefully, by virtue of the responsibilities associated with specific positions, which faculty and staff needed to be designated as mandatory reporters. Rather than undertaking such a time-intensive process, many colleges and universities opted for the blanket policy, which was not only simpler, but ensured that they could not find themselves in disagreement with the OCR about whether they had correctly determined their list of mandatory reporters" (3).
13. See the introduction for a discussion of our language, which draws on decades of feminist and queer activism and advocacy.

## Chapter 2: Stepping Up in a Safe Haven

1. In one of Foubert's studies, 6 percent of men in fraternities who completed the Men's Program reported behavior that constitutes sexual assault, whereas 10 percent of men in fraternities who did not complete the training reported behavior constituting sexual assault (Foubert, Newberry, and Tatum, 2007). In another study, women reported being more protective of their friends after completing the Women's Program (Foubert and Perry, 2007).
2. See: Foubert (2000); Foubert (2011b); Foubert and Cowell (2004); Foubert, Godin, and Tatum (2010); Foubert, Langhinrichsen-Rohling, Brasfield, and Hill (2010); Foubert and La Voy (2000); Foubert and Marriott (1997); Foubert and McEwen (1998); Foubert and Newberry (2006); Foubert, Newberry, and Tatum (2007); Foubert and Perry (2007); Foubert, Tatum, and Godin (2010).
3. The second author attended a presentation of the Men's Program as an undergraduate (circa 2006) and asked this question privately when the speakers made themselves available for one-on-one conversations. The presenter gave a rote response to the question in order to indicate empirical support for the

claim that the police training video has not been found to foment homophobia among audience members.

4. Antiviolence educator Jackson Katz warns that bystander intervention tips are often superficial and ineffective (Israelsen-Hartley 2016). He founded Mentors in Violence Prevention (MVP) in order to develop and disseminate bystander-intervention education based in dismantling gender norms such as toxic masculinity. See MVP Strategies (2015).

5. In the course of training, Haven collects aggregate data about students in order to make claims about college students' behavioral norms. So while Everfi profits from our students as "consumers" of their "product," they also use our students' data to revise their training and generate more profit.

6. The analysis of Timpf's presentation is based on the second author's detailed notes he took when he attended the talk. Although Timpf passed around a signup sheet so that audience members could get a copy of her presentation, the second author never received the promised email. The presentation is thus not cited in a traditional way because it is not retrievable.

## Chapter 3: Consent Goes Viral

1 . Later in the same chapter, hooks quotes feminist Ellen Willis, who writes (and we agree): "From a radical standpoint, . . . sexual liberation involves not only the abolition of restrictions but the positive presence of social and psychological conditions that foster satisfying sexual relations" (149).

2. See https://everydayfeminism.com/2015/06/how-society-treats-consent/ for the cartoon.

3. Here we acknowledge Kristy Maddux's (2009) point that media artifacts may function as fruitful pedagogical tools, even (or especially) as we critique their shortcomings or analyze some of their entailments. We resist the temptation to create a binary where we must demonize that which we critique. Indeed, throughout this book we critique some of what we value most because we care about making it better.

4. This campaign started in 2010 (part 1) and continued in 2012 (part 2). Full versions of each PSA appear on the campaign's website, where users are free to download or share the images (SAVE 2010, 2012).

5. See chapter 1 for a fuller discussion of patterns of gender violence.

6. In their 2013 study of adolescent perpetration of sexual violence, published in the *Journal of the American Medical Association*, Ybarra and Mitchell clarify the importance of defining sexual violence more broadly:

> Some may argue that the definitions of rape and sexual assault in our investigation are too broad. Indeed, this may be why the perpetration rate among females is higher than might be posited. Rape includes acts beyond those in which the victim is physically overpowered,

however. Restrictive definitions have potentially led to undercounting of sexual assault experiences. For example, in the National Violence Against Women Survey, respondents were asked whether anyone had ever made them engage in a sexual activity "by using force or threat of force." Psychological coercion was not clearly specified even though there are multiple coercive strategies other than physical force that can be used in a rape. To ensure that comprehensive rates of sexual assault and rape are identified as well as to begin building the research base on female perpetrators, research needs to include a fuller spectrum of rape scenarios. (1132)

## Chapter 4: Trigger Warnings as Holistic Consent

1. By "safe space," what we mean is precisely not refuge from new ideas or ideas with which students disagree. Instead, we mean spaces in which students are free to explore their own views about a topic, including disagreeing with each other and with a professor, as long as they do not engage in willful hate speech or character attacks. In a safe space, students (and faculty!) are not shielded from the world but are instead invited into it, with the chance to grow and expand based on respectful conversation and feedback.

2. In a related point, Rebecca Stringer (2016) highlights that trigger warning equivalents exist in other contexts without controversy. For example, before medical students work on cadavers for the first time, they receive training about emotional boundaries. We would add that in all manner of helping professions (social workers, counselors, clergy), training in boundaries and self-care functions as a routine and thoroughly necessary part of the work people do in their preparatory education and in continuing education seminars.

3. In our view, inviting students to participate in constructing course readings is often good pedagogical practice. For more on this argument, see chapter 5.

4. In the context of the #MeToo movement—which began one year after Goldberg's essay was published and the year in which Trump took office—this argument strikes us as particularly reprehensible (if common among critics of #MeToo). It is interesting that the same argument against trigger warnings is made against women speaking out about the experience of sexual harassment and violence. See Zacharek, Dockterman, and Sweetland Edwards (2017). For early scholarly takes on the #MeToo movement, see Barker (2018), Battaglia, Edley, and Newsom (2019), and Larabee (2018).

## Chapter 5: Survivor-Centered Pedagogy

1. This statistic (11.2 percent) includes undergraduate and graduate students. See Cantor et al. (2015).

2. We discuss accessibility and intellectual consent in detail in chapter 4.

3. See the introduction for a fuller discussion of Gilmore (2017) and Manne (2018).

4. We are indebted to Tristan Booth for the idea of calling only the last names on the roster and allowing students to provide the first name they use. Booth's strategy and other ideas for centering the needs of trans students in classrooms appear in Capuzza et al. (forthcoming). See also, Catalano (2015); Jourian, Simmons, and Devaney (2016); Malatino (2015); Nicolazzo (2016); Platero and Harsin (2015); Spencer and Capuzza (2016).

5. See chapter 1 for a critique of the Clery Act and our university's crime alerts concerning sexual violence.

6. For compelling scholarly treatments of neoliberalism, see Brown (2015); Harvey (2007); and Mohanty (2013). See the introduction for our discussion of neoliberalism in higher education.

7. For more on consumer media feminism (or "postfeminism"), see especially Gill and Scharrf (2011), McRobbie (2004), Owen (1999), and Tasker and Negra (2007).

8. Examples of such counternarratives include, in addition to the texts discussed below, Dorothy Allison's *Two or Three Things I Know for Sure* (1996) and *Bastard Out of Carolina* (1992); Kiese Laymon's *Heavy: An American Memoir* (2018); Toni Morrison's *The Bluest Eye* (1970); Louise Erdrich's *The Round House* (2012); and Terese Marie Mailhot's *Heart Berries: A Memoir* (2018), among others. Our arguments in this book are indebted to those survivors who have put the complexity of their stories into words and who have made connections among individual trauma, collective trauma, and the precarity and vulnerability of poverty, racialized and gendered violence, and mental illness.

9. For an analysis of Shailja Patel's *Migritude* in the context of neoliberal human rights movements and markets, see Kulbaga (2016).

10. It is perhaps clearer how such an approach might apply in a humanities or social sciences course, but we believe that it is also useful, for example, in a statistics class when discussing violence; in an economics class when discussing poverty and discrimination; and in an art history class when discussing images of rape or lynching.

## Conclusion: Cultivating Campuses of Consent

1. Given the high-profile cases of alleged sexual assault and harassment in higher education that have renewed conversations about the boundaries between faculty and students, such nostalgia is particularly unfortunate. See Joshua Trey Barnett (2019), Andrea Long Chu (2018), Lili Loofbourow (2018), and the poet Shreerekha (2018) for analyses of the Avital Ronell and Junot Díaz cases.

2. See Manne (2018) for a discussion of epistemic oppression and the various

forms silencing can take, including *testimonial smothering* (Dotson 2011), "which denotes a kind of self-silencing on the part of the speaker . . . due to it being unsafe or risky to make certain claims, likely futile anyway" (Manne 2018, 4–7).

3. Both of us are White and cisgender, and perhaps most important in this moment, we are confidently and safely employed as tenured faculty members. We move through the world with White privilege and class privilege. One of us experiences male privilege but also homophobia, while one of us faces sexism yet enjoys heterosexual privilege. We both have places to live, food to eat, and little fear that making these critiques (in an email to an administrator, at a heated face-to-face meeting, or in a published book) will result in a canceled contract or any form of economic retribution.

4. Ahmed's (2012, 2017) past work on institutional critique has been foundational to this project, and we very much anticipate her work on complaint (2018), which addresses what stories about sexual harassment, violence, and discrimination reveal about how power operates on campus.

5. For a small sampling of these arguments, see Berg and Seeber (2016); Spencer and Patterson (2017); Springer (2016); Wagner, Kulbaga, and Cohen (2017).

6. We are indebted to (and inspired by!) Karma Chávez (2010) for the observation that norms imply other possibilities.

# REFERENCES

Agosín, Marjorie. 2002. *Women, Gender, and Human Rights: A Global Perspective*. New Brunswick, NJ: Rutgers University Press.

Ahmed, Sara. 2010. "Happy Objects." In *The Affect Theory Reader*, edited by Melissa Gregg and Gregory J. Seigworth, 29–51. Durham, NC: Duke University Press.

——. 2012. *On Being Included: Racism and Diversity in Institutional Life*. Durham, NC: Duke University Press.

——. 2016. "Resignation is a Feminist Issue." *feministkilljoys*. August 27, 2016. https://feministkilljoys.com/2016/08/27/resignation-is-a-feminist-issue/.

——. 2017. *Living a Feminist Life*. Durham, NC: Duke University Press.

——. 2018. "Complaint." *Sara Ahmed*. https://www.saranahmed.com/complaint/

Alcoff, Linda Martín. 2018. *Rape and Resistance*. Cambridge, UK: Polity Press.

Alexander, Michelle. 2012. *The New Jim Crow: Mass Incarceration in the Age of Colorblindness*. New York: The New Press.

Allen, Brenda J. 1996. "Feminist Standpoint Theory: A Black Woman's (Re)view of Organizational Socialization." *Communication Studies* 47 (4): 257–71. https://doi.org/10.1080/10510979609368482.

Allison, Dorothy. 1992. *Bastard Out of Carolina: A Novel*. New York: Plume.

——. 1995. *Two or Three Things I Know for Sure*. New York: Plume.

Anderson, Linda A., and Susan C. Whiston. 2005. "Sexual Assault Education Programs: A Meta-Analytic Examination of Their Effectiveness." *Psychology of Women Quarterly* 29: 374–88.

Anderson, Michelle J. 2016. "Campus Sexual Assault Adjudication and Resistance to Reform." *Yale Law Journal* 125:1940–2005.

Anker, Ashley E., and Thomas Hugh Feeley. 2011. "Asking the Difficult Questions: Message Strategies Used by Organ Procurement Coordinators in Requesting Familial Consent to Organ Donation." *Journal of Health Communication* 16 (6): 643–59. https://doi.org/10.1080/10810730.2011.551999.

Archard, David. 2007. "The Wrong of Rape." *Philosophical Quarterly* 57:374–93. https://doi.org/10.1111/j.1467–9213.2007.492.x.

Association of American Universities (AAU). 2015. "AAU Campus Climate Survey on Sexual Assault and Sexual Misconduct." https://www.aau.edu/Climate-Survey.aspx?id=16525.

*Audrie & Daisy.* 2016. Bonni Cohen and Jon Shenk. Netflix, 2016. Film.

Baker, Katie J. M. 2016. "Here Is The Powerful Letter The Stanford Victim Read Aloud To Her Attacker." *BuzzFeed.* June 3, 2016. https://www.buzzfeed.com/katiejmbaker/heres-the-powerful-letter-the-stanford-victim-read-to-her-ra?utm_term=.ts3KVY2er#.vgglYzyb6.

Barker, Justin L. 2018. "The #MeToo Movement and Ovid's Philomela." *Radical Teacher* 110 (Winter): 65–67. https://doi.org/10.5195/rt.2018.447.

Barnett, Joshua Trey. 2015. "Fleshy Metamorphosis: Temporal Pedagogies of Transsexual Counterpublics." In *Transgender Communication Studies: Histories, Trends, and Trajectories,* edited by Leland G. Spencer and Jamie C. Capuzza, 155–69. Lanham, MD: Lexington Books.

——. 2019. "A Certain Fidelity to Infidelity: Thinking Against Loyalty in the Academy." *Women & Language* 42 (1): 145–50. https://doi.org/10.34046/WL.2019.015.

Barone, Ryan P., Jennifer R. Wolgemuth, and Chris Linder. 2007. "Preventing Sexual Assault Through Engaging College Men." *Journal of College Student Development* 48 (5): 585–94. https://doi.org/10.1353/csd.2007.0045.

Battaglia, Judy E., Paige P. Edley, and Victoria Ann Newsom. 2019. "Intersectional Feminisms and Sexual Violence in the Era of Me Too, Trump, and Kavanaugh." *Women & Language* 42 (1): 133–44. https://doi.org/10.34046/WL.2019.014.

Bauer, Robin. 2014. *Queer BDSM Intimacies: Critical Consent and Pushing Boundaries.* New York: Palgrave MacMillan.

Berg, Maggie, and Barbara Seeber. 2016. *The Slow Professor: Challenging the Culture of Speed in the Academy.* Toronto: University of Toronto Press.

Berkowitz, Alan D. 2002. "A Response from John Foubert." http://www.alanberkowitz.com/foubert_response.html.

Berlant, Lauren. 1997. *The Queen of America Goes to Washington City: Essays on Sex and Citizenship.* Durham: Duke University Press.

——. 2008. *The Female Complaint: The Unfinished Business of Sentimentality in American Culture.* Durham: Duke University Press.

Bissonnette, Jean François, and Christian Laval. 2017. "Gambling with 'Human Capital': on the Speculative Logic of the 'Knowledge Economy.'" *World Social and Economic Review* 8 (April). http://wer.worldeconomicsassociation.org/files/WEA-WSER-8-Bissonnette-Laval.pdf.

Bluhm, Alyssa. 2016. "Tickling or Torture: What It Teaches Us About Consent." *Catcall.* June 29, 2016. https://catcallmag.wordpress.com/2016/06/29/tickling-or-torture-what-it-teaches-us-about-consent/.

Boler, Megan. 1999. *Feeling Power: Emotions and Education.* London: Routledge.

Bone, Jennifer Emerling, Cindy L. Griffin, and T. M. Linda Scholz. 2008.

"Beyond Traditional Conceptualizations of Rhetoric: Invitational Rhetoric and a Move toward Civility." *Western Journal of Communication* 72 (October): 434–62.

Boston Women's Health Book Collective. 1976. *Our Bodies, Ourselves: A Book By and For Women*. New York: Touchstone.

Boux, Holly Jeanine, and Courtenay W. Daum. 2015. "At the Intersection of Social Media and Rape Culture: How Facebook Postings, Texting and Other Personal Communications Challenge the Real Rape Myth in the Criminal Justice System." *Journal of Law, Technology & Policy* 2015 (1): 149–86.

Boyer, John W. 2002. *Academic Freedom and the Modern University: The Experience of the University of Chicago*. Chicago: The College of the University of Chicago.

Boysen, Guy A., Anna Mae Wells, and Kaylee J. Dawson. 2016. "Instructors' Use of Trigger Warnings and Behavior Warnings in Abnormal Psychology." *Teaching of Psychology* 43 (4): 334–39. https://doi.org/10.1177/0098628316662766.

Brown, Megan C. 2013. "Learning to Live Again: Contemporary US Memoir as Biopolitical Self Care Guide." *Biography* 36, no. 2 (Spring): 359–75.

Brown, Ruth Nicole. 2009. *Black Girlhood Celebration: Toward a Hip-Hop Feminist Pedagogy*. New York: Peter Lang.

Brown, Wendy. 2015. *Undoing the Demos: Neoliberalism's Stealth Revolution*. New York: Zone Books.

Brownmiller, Susan. 1975. *Against Our Will: Men, Women, and Rape*. New York: Simon and Schuster.

Burgess, Jean. 2008. "'All Your Chocolate Rain Are Belong to Us'? Viral Video, YouTube, and the Dynamics of Participatory Culture." In *Video Vortex Reader: Responses to YouTube*, edited by Geert Lovink and Sabine Niederer, 101–9. Amsterdam: Institute of Network Cultures.

Burke, Kenneth. 1959. *Attitudes toward History*. 2nd ed. Los Altos, CA: Hermes Publications.

——. 1966. *Language as Symbolic Action: Essays on Life, Literature, and Method*. Berkeley: University of California Press.

——. 1984. *Permanence and Change: An Anatomy of Purpose*. Berkeley: University of California Press.

Burke, Penny Jane. 2015. "Re/imagining Higher Education Pedagogies: Gender, Emotion and Difference." *Teaching in Higher Education* 20 (4): 388–401.

Cahill, Ann. Forthcoming. "Disclosing an Experience of Sexual Assault: Ethics and the Role of the Confidant." In *Vulnerability and the Politics of Care: Cross-Disciplinary Dialogues*, edited by Doerthe Rosenow, Victoria Browne, and Jason Danely. Oxford: Oxford University Press.

Campbell, Peter Odell, and Cory Holding. 2015. "The Trans-Exclusive Archive of U.S. Capital Punishment Rhetoric." In *Transgender Communication Studies:*

*Histories, Trends, and Trajectories*, edited by Leland G. Spencer and Jamie C. Capuzza, 199–216. Lanham, MD: Lexington Books.

Cantor, David, Bonnie Fisher, Susan Chibnall, Reanne Townsend, Hyunshik Lee, Carol Bruce, and Gail Thomas. 2015. "Report on the AAU Campus Climate Survey on Sexual Assault and Sexual Misconduct," Association of American Universities (AAU). September 21, 2015. https://www.aau.edu/key-issues/aau-climate-survey-sexual-assault-and-sexual-misconduct-2015.

Capuzza, Jamie C., Leland G. Spencer, Thomas J. Billard, E. Tristan Booth, matthew heinz, Sarah Jones, and Lucy J. Miller. Forthcoming. "Transing Communication Education: A Chorus of Voices." In *Queer Communication Pedagogy*, edited by Ahmet Atay and Sandra Pensoneau-Conway.

Card, Claudia. 1996. "Rape as a Weapon of War." *Hypatia* 11 (4): 5–18. https://doi.org/10.1111/j.1527-2001.1996.tb01031.x.

Carlson, Melanie. 2008. "I'd Rather Go Along and Be Considered A Man: Masculinity and Bystander Intervention." *The Journal of Men's Studies* 16 (1): 3–17. https://doi.org/10.3149/jms.1601.3.

Carter, Angela M. 2015. "Teaching with Trauma: Disability Pedagogy, Feminism, and the Trigger Warnings Debate." *Disability Studies Quarterly* 35 (2). https://doi.org/10.18061/dsq.v35i2.4652.

Catalano, D. Chase J. 2015. "'Trans Enough?': The Pressures Trans Men Negotiate in Higher Education." *TSQ: Transgender Studies Quarterly* 2 (3): 411–30. https://doi.org/10.1215/23289252-2926399.

Chafetz, Janet Saltzman. 1997. "Feminist Theory and Sociology: Underutilized Contributions for Mainstream Theory." *Annual Review of Sociology* 23: 97–120.

Chapleau, Kristine M., and Debra L. Oswald. 2014. "A System Justification View of Sexual Violence: Legitimizing Gender Inequality and Reduced Moral Outrage Are Connected to Greater Rape Myth Acceptance." *Journal of Trauma & Dissociation* 15 (2): 204–18. https://doi.org/10.1080/15299732.2014.867573.

Chávez, Karma R. 2010. "Spatializing Gender Performativity: Ecstasy and Possibilities for Livable Life in the Tragic Case of Victoria Arellano." *Women's Studies in Communication* 33 (1): 1–15. https://doi.org/10.1080/07491401003669729.

Chu, Andrea Long. 2018. "I Worked with Avital Ronell. I Believe Her Accuser." *The Chronicle of Higher Education*. August 30, 2018. https://www.chronicle.com/article/I-Worked-With-Avital-Ronell-I/244415.

Clark, Annie E., and Andrea L. Pino. 2016. *We Believe You: Survivors of Campus Sexual Assault Speak Out*. New York: Holt.

Clery Center. 2017. "Summary of the Jeanne Clery Act." https://clerycenter.org/policy-resources/the-clery-act/.

Coulter, Robert W. S., and Susan R. Rankin. 2017. "College Sexual Assault and Campus Climate for Sexual- and Gender-Minority Undergraduate Students." *Journal of Interpersonal Violence*. https://doi.org/10.1177/0886260517696870.

Davis, Angela Y. 1981. "Rape, Racism and the Capitalist Setting." *The Black Scholar* 12 (6): 39–45. https://doi.org/10.1080/00064246.1981.11414219.

——. 1983. *Women, Race, and Class.* New York: Random House.

Davis, Corey B., Mark Glantz, and David R. Novak. 2016. "'You Can't Run Your SUV on Cute. Let's Go!': Internet Memes as Delegitimizing Discourse." *Environmental Communication* 10 (1): 62–83. https://doi.org/10.1080/175240 32.2014.991411.

Deer, Sarah. 2015. *The Beginning and End of Rape: Confronting Sexual Violence in Native America.* Minneapolis: University of Minnesota Press.

DeLuca, Kevin Michael. 2006. "The Speed of Immanent Images: The Dangers of Reading Photographs." In *Visual Communication: Perception, Rhetoric, and Technology,* edited by Diane S. Hope, 79–90. Cresskill, NJ: Hampton Press.

DeMatteo, David, Meghann Galloway, Shelby Arnold, and Unnati Patel. 2015. "Sexual Assault on College Campuses: A 50-State Survey of Criminal Sexual Assault Statutes and Their Relevance to Campus Sexual Assault." *Psychology, Public Policy, and Law* 21 (3): 227–38. https://doi.org/10.1037/law0000055.

D'Enbeau, Suzy. 2017. "Unpacking the Dimensions of Organizational Tension: The Case of Sexual Violence Response and Prevention among College Students." *Journal of Applied Communication Research* 45 (3): 237–55. https://doi.org/10.1080/00909882.2017.1320568.

Deschamps, Marie, Hassan B. Jallow, and Yasmin Sooka. 2015. *Taking Action on Sexual Exploitation and Abuse by Peacekeepers: Report of an Independent Review on Sexual Exploitation and Abuse by International Peacekeeping Forces in the Central African Republic.* December 17, 2015. https://www.un.org/News/dh/infocus/centafricrepub/Independent-Review-Report.pdf.

Dewey, Caitlin. 2016. "6 in 10 of You Will Share This Link without Reading It, a New, Depressing Study Says" *Washington Post.* June 16, 2016. https://www.washingtonpost.com/news/the-intersect/wp/2016/06/16/six-in-10-of-you-will-share-this-link-without-reading-it-according-to-a-new-and-depressing-study/?noredirect=on&utm_term=.bd138ffff29a.

Dingo, Rebecca. 2012. *Networking Arguments: Rhetoric, Transnational Feminism, and Public Policy Writing.* Pittsburgh: University of Pittsburgh Press.

Dobbin, Frank, and Alexandra Kalev. 2016. "Why Diversity Programs Fail." July/August. https://hbr.org/2016/07/why-diversity-programs-fail.

Donoghue, Frank. 2008. *The Last Professors: The Corporate University and the End of the Humanities.* New York: Fordham University Press.

Dotson, Kristie. 2011. "Tracking Epistemic Violence, Tracking Practices of Silence." *Hypatia: A Journal of Feminist Philosophy* 26 (2): 236–57. https://doi.org/10.1111/j.1527-2001.2011.01177.x.

Dow, Bonnie J. 2001. "*Ellen,* Television, and the Politics of Gay and Lesbian Visibility." *Critical Studies in Media Communication* 18 (2): 123–40.

Duerringer, Christopher M. 2016. "Who Would Jesus Bomb? The Republican Jesus Meme and the Fracturing of Ideology." *Social Media + Society* 2 (1): 1–12. https://doi.org/10.1177/2056305116637095.

Duggan, Lisa. 2004. *The Twilight of Equality?* Boston: Beacon Press.

Ehrlich, Susan. 2001. *Representing Rape: Language and Sexual Consent*. New York: Routledge.

Ellsworth, Elizabeth. 1989. "Why Doesn't This Feel Empowering? Working through the Repressive Myths of Critical Pedagogy." *Harvard Educational Review* 59 (3): 297–324. https://doi.org/0017–8055/89/0800–0297.

Enloe, Cynthia. 2004. *The Curious Feminist: Searching for Women in a New Age of Empire*. Berkeley: University of California Press.

Erdrich, Louise. 2012. *The Round House: A Novel*. New York: Harper Perennial.

Everfi. 2014. "Everfi Fact Sheet." January 2014. http://info.everfi.com/rs/everfi/images/EverFi%20Fact%20Sheet%20-%20 Updated%20January%202014.pdf.

Fahlberg, Anjuli, and Pepper, Mollie. (2016) "Masculinity and Sexual Violence: Assessing the State of the Field." *Sociology Compass* 10: 673–83. http://doi.org/10.1111/soc4.12397.

Fantz, Ashley. 2016. "Outrage over 6-Month Sentence for Brock Turner in Stanford Rape Case." *CNN*. June 7, 2016. http://www.cnn.com/2016/06/06/ us/sexual-assault-brock-turner-stanford/index.html.

Fawaz, Ramzi. 2016. "Locked Eyes." *QED: A Journal in GLBTQ Worldmaking* 3 (3): a138–41.

Fenton, Natalie. 2011. "Deregulation or Democracy? New Media, News, Neoliberalism and the Public Interest." *Continuum: Journal of Media & Cultural Studies* 25 (1): 63–72. https://doi.org/10.1080/10304312.2011.539159.

Ferree, Myra Marx, and Beth B. Hess. 1994. *Controversy and Coalition: The New Feminist Movement across Three Decades of Change*. New York: Twayne.

Filipovic, Jill. 2017. "Two Books Explore the Furor Over Rape on Campus." *The New York Times*. April 7, 2017. https://www.nytimes.com/2017/04/07/ books/review/two-books-explore-the-furor-over-rape-on-campus.html.

Firestone, Shulamith. 1970. *The Dialectic of Sex*. New York: William Morrow.

Fischel, Joseph. 2019. *Screw Consent: A Better Politics of Sexual Justice*. Berkeley: University of California Press.

Fitzgerald, Louise F., Linda L. Collinsworth, and Melanie S. Harned. 2001. "Sexual Harassment." In *Encyclopedia of Women and Gender*, 2: 991–1004. San Diego: Academic Press.

Ford, Jessie, and José G. Soto-Marquez. 2016. "Sexual Assault Victimization Among Straight, Gay/Lesbian, and Bisexual College Students." *Violence and Gender* 3 (2): 107–15. https://doi.org/10.1089/vio.2015.0030.

Foss, Sonja K., and Cindy L. Griffin. 1995. "Beyond Persuasion: A Proposal for an Invitational Rhetoric." *Communication Monographs* 62 (March): 2–18.

Foubert, John D. 2000. "The Longitudinal Effects of a Rape-Prevention Program on Fraternity Men's Attitudes, Behavioral Intent, and Behavior." *Journal of American College Health* 48: 158–63.

—. 2002. "The Truth About 'Are Foubert's Claims About "The Men's Program" Overstated.'" http://www.alanberkowitz.com/foubert_response.html.

—. 2011a. "Answering the Questions of Rape Prevention Research: A Response to Tharp et al. (2011)." *Journal of Interpersonal Violence* 26 (16): 3393–402. https://doi.org/10.1177/0886260511416480.

—. 2011b. *The Men's and Women's Programs: Ending Rape through Peer Education.* New York: Routledge.

Foubert, John D., and Edwin A. Cowell. 2004. "Perceptions of a Rape Prevention Program by Fraternity Men and Male Student Athletes: Powerful Effects and Implications for Changing Behavior." *NASPA Journal* 42 (1): 1–20.

Foubert, John D., and Brandynne J. Cremedy. 2007. "Reactions of Men of Color to a Commonly Used Rape Prevention Program: Attitude and Predicted Behavior Changes." *Sex Roles* 57 (1–2): 137–44. https://doi.org/10.1007/s11199-007-9216-2.

Foubert, John D., Eric E. Godin, and Jerry L. Tatum. 2010. "In Their Own Words: Sophomore College Men Describe Attitude and Behavior Changes Resulting From a Rape Prevention Program 2 Years After Their Participation." *Journal of Interpersonal Violence* 25 (12): 2237–57. https://doi.org/10.1177/0886260509354881.

Foubert, John D., Jennifer Langhinrichsen-Rohling, Hope Brasfield, and Brent Hill. 2010. "Effects of a Rape Awareness Program on College Women: Increasing Bystander Efficacy and Willingness to Intervene." *Journal of Community Psychology* 38 (7): 813–27. https://doi.org/10.1002/jcop.20397.

Foubert, John D., and Sharon A. La Voy. 2000. "A Qualitative Assessment of 'The Men's Program': The Impact of a Rape Prevention Program on Fraternity Men." *NASPA Journal* 38 (1): 18–30.

Foubert, John D., and Kenneth A. Marriott. 1997. "Effects of a Sexual Assault Peer Education Program on Men's Belief in Rape Myths." *Sex Roles* 36 (3/4): 259–68.

Foubert, John D., and Marylu K. McEwan. 1998. "An All-Male Rape Prevention Peer Education Program: Decreasing Fraternity Men's Behavioral Intent to Rape." *Journal of College Student Development* 39 (6): 548–56.

Foubert, John D., and Jonathan T. Newberry. 2006. "Effects of Two Versions of an Empathy-Based Rape Prevention Program on Fraternity Men's Survivor Empathy, Attitudes, and Behavioral Intent to Commit Rape or Sexual Assault." *Journal of College Student Development* 47 (2): 133–48.

Foubert, John D., Jonathan T. Newberry, and Jerry L. Tatum. 2007. "Behavior Differences Seven Months Later: Effects of a Rape Prevention Program." *NASPA Journal* 44 (4): 728–49.

Foubert, John D., and Bradford C. Perry. 2007. "Creating Lasting Attitude and Behavior Change in Fraternity Members and Male Student Athletes: The

Qualitative Impact of an Empathy-Based Rape Prevention Program." *Violence Against Women* 13 (1): 70–86. https://doi. org/10.1177/1077801206295125.

Foubert, John D., Jerry L. Tatum, and Eric E. Godin. 2010. "First-Year Male Students' Perceptions of a Rape Prevention Program 7 Months after Their Participation: Attitude and Behavior Changes." *Journal of College Student Development* 51 (6): 707–15.

Freire, Paolo. 1970. *Pedagogy of the Oppressed*. New York: Bloomsbury Academic Press Reissue.

Freitag, Jennifer L. 2018. "Four Transgressive Declarations for Ending Gender Violence." In *Transgressing Feminist Theory and Discourse: Advancing Conversations across Disciplines*, edited by Jennifer C. Dunn and Jimmie Manning, 134–50. New York: Routledge.

Fricker, Miranda. 2009. *Epistemic Injustice: Power and the Ethics of Knowing*. Oxford: Oxford UP.

Gardner, Lee. 2015. "25 Years Later, Has Clery Made Campuses Safer?" *The Chronicle of Higher Education*. March 9, 2015. https://www.chronicle.com/ article/25-Years-Later-Has-Clery/228305.

Gay, Roxane, ed. 2018. *Not That Bad: Dispatches from Rape Culture*. New York: HarperCollins.

Gill, Rosalind. 2016. "Post-postfeminism?: New Feminist Visibilities in Postfeminist Times." *Feminist Media Studies*, 16 (4): 610–30. https://doi.org/1 0.1080/14680777.2016.1193293.

Gill, Rosalind, and Christina Scharrf. 2011. *New Femininities: Postfeminism, Neoliberalism and Subjectivity*. New York: Palgrave Macmillan.

Gilmore, Leigh. 2010. "American Neoconfessional: Memoir, Self-Help, and Redemption on Oprah's Couch." *Biography* 33 (4): 657–79.

——. 2017. *Tainted Witness: Why We Doubt What Women Say About Their Lives*. New York: Columbia University Press.

Goldberg, Erica. 2016. "Free Speech Consequentialism." *Columbia Law Review* 116: 687–756.

Gotell, Lise. 2008. "Rethinking Affirmative Consent in Canadian Sexual Assault Law: Neoliberal Sexual Subjects and Risky Women." *Akron Law Review* 41, no. 4 Article 3. http://ideaexchange.uakron.edu/akronlawreview/vol41/iss4/3.

Grewal, Inderpal. 2005. *Transnational America: Feminisms, Diasporas, Neoliberalisms*. Durham: Duke University Press.

Griffin, Vanessa Woodward, Dylan Pelletier, O. Hayden Griffin, and John J. Sloan. 2017. "Campus Sexual Violence Elimination Act: SaVing Lives or SaVing Face?" *American Journal of Criminal Justice* 42 (2): 401–25. https://doi.org/10.1007/s12103-016-9356-4.

Grigoriadis, Vanessa. 2017. *Blurred Lines: Rethinking Sex, Power, & Consent on Campus*. Boston: Houghton Mifflin Harcourt.

Gross, Ken, and Andrea Fine. 1990. "After Their Daughter Is Murdered at College, Her Grieving Parents Mount a Crusade for Campus Safety." *People.* February 19, 1990. http://people.com/archive/after-their-daughter-is-murdered-at-college-her-grieving-parents-mount-a-crusade-for-campus-safety-vol-33-no-7/.

Guest Pryal, Katie Rose. 2015. "Raped on Campus? Don't Trust Your College to Do the Right Thing." *The Chronicle.* March 2, 2015. http://www.chronicle.com/article/Raped-on-Campus-Don-t-Trust/228093.

Guffey, James. 2013. "Crime on Campus: Can Clery Act Data from Universities and Colleges be Trusted?" *American Society of Business and Behavioral Sciences eJournal* 9 (1): 51–61.

Hahner, Leslie A. 2013. "The Riot Kiss: Framing Memes as Visual Argument." *Argumentation & Advocacy* 49: 151–66.

Halberstam, Jack. 2017. "Trigger Happy: From Content Warning to Censorship." *Signs: Journal of Women in Culture & Society* 42 (2): 535–42.

Halterman, Aaron W., Nicole T. Gabana, and Jesse A. Steinfeldt. 2017. "Multiculturalism in Sport Psychology Practice: Perspectives and Experiences of Trainees." In *The Peer Guide to Applied Sport Psychology for Consultants in Training*, edited by Mark W. Aoyagi, Artur Poczwardowski, and Jamie L. Shapiro, 149–62. New York: Routledge.

Harding, Sandra G. 1991. *Whose Science? Whose Knowledge?: Thinking from Women's Lives.* Ithaca, NY: Cornell University Press.

Harrington, Carol. 2010. *Politicization of Sexual Violence: From Abolitionism to Peacekeeping.* New York: Routledge.

Harris, Kate Lockwood. 2011. "The Next Problem with No Name: The Politics and Pragmatics of the Word Rape." *Women's Studies in Communication* 34 (1): 42–63. https://doi.org/10.1080/07491409.2011.566533.

———. 2017. "Re-situating Organizational Knowledge: Violence, Intersectionality and the Privilege of Partial Perspective." *Human Relations* 70 (3): 263–85. https://doi.org/10.1177/0018726716654745.

———. 2018. "Yes Means Yes and No Means No, but Both These Mantras Need to Go: Communication Myths in Consent Education and Anti-Rape Activism." *Journal of Applied Communication Research* 46 (2): 155–78. https://doi.org/10.1080/00909882.2018.1435900.

———. 2019. *Beyond the Rapist: Title IX and Sexual Violence on US Campuses.* New York: Oxford University Press.

Harvey, David. 2007. *A Brief History of Neoliberalism.* London: Oxford University Press.

Hasinoff, Amy Adele. 2015. *Sexting Panic: Rethinking Criminalization, Privacy, and Consent.* Urbana: University of Illinois Press.

Henderson, Lynne N. 1987. "What Makes Rape a Crime." *Berkeley Women's Law Journal* 3: 193–229.

Hesford, Wendy S. 2011. *Spectacular Rhetorics: Human Rights Visions, Recognitions, Feminisms.* Durham, NC: Duke University Press.

Hesford, Wendy S., Adela C. Licona, and Christa Teston, eds. 2018. *Precarious Rhetorics*. Columbus, OH: The Ohio State University Press.

Hickey, Jeremiah. 2016. "Exempting the University: Trigger Warnings and Intellectual Space." *First Amendment Studies* 50 (2): 70–82. https://doi.org/10.1080/21689725.2016.1233073.

Higate, Paul. 2007. "Peacekeepers, Masculinities, and Sexual Exploitation." *Men and Masculinities* 10.1: 99–119. https://doi.org/10.1177/1097184X06291896.

Higate, Paul, and Marsha Henry. 2004. "Engendering (In)security in Peace Support Operations." *Security Dialogue* 35. 4: 481–98. https://doi.org/10.1177/0967010604049529.

Hill Collins, Patricia. 2004. *Black Sexual Politics: African Americans, Gender, and the New Racism*. New York: Routledge.

Hockett, Jericho M., Donald A. Saucier, Bethany H. Hoffman, Sara J. Smith, and Adam W. Craig. 2009. "Oppression Through Acceptance?: Predicting Rape Myth Acceptance and Attitudes Toward Rape Victims." *Violence Against Women* 15 (8):877–97. https://doi.org/10.1177/1077801209335489.

hooks, bell. 1994. *Teaching to Transgress: Education as the Practice of Freedom*. New York: Routledge.

——. 2000. *Feminist Theory: From Margin to Center*. 2nd ed. Cambridge, MA: South End Press.

——. 2015. *Feminist Theory: From Margin to Center*. 3rd ed. New York: Routledge.

*Hunting Ground, The*. 2015. Kirby Dick. The Weinstein Company, 2015. Film.

Huntington, Heidi E. 2016. "Pepper Spray Cop and the American Dream: Using Synecdoche and Metaphor to Unlock Internet Memes' Visual Political Rhetoric." *Communication Studies* 67 (1): 77–93. https://doi.org/10.1080/10510974.2015.1087414.

*Invisible War, The*. 2012. Kirby Dick. Chain Camera Pictures, 2012. Film.

Israelsen-Hartley, Sara. 2016. "The Power of Bystanders to End Rape Culture." *Deseret News*. August 16, 2016. http://www.jacksonkatz.com/news/the-power-of-bystanders-to-end-rape-culture/.

It's On Us. 2018. "Videos." http://www.itsonus.org/videos/.

Ivy, Diana K. 2016. "College Students' Sexual Safety: The Verbal and Nonverbal Communication of Consent." In *Contemporary Studies of Sexuality and Communication: Theoretical and Applied Perspectives*, edited by Jimmie Manning and Carey Noland, 405–18. Dubuque, IA: Kendall Hunt.

Iyama, Karri. 2012. "'We Have Tolled the Bell for Him': An Analysis of the Prison Rape Elimination Act and California's Compliance as It Applies to Transgender Inmates." *Law & Sexuality: A Review of Lesbian, Gay, Bisexual & Transgender Legal Issues* 21 (April): 23–48.

Janosik, Steven M., and Donald D. Gehring. 2003. "The Impact of the Clery Campus Crime Disclosure Act on Student Behavior." *Journal of College Student Development* 44 (1): 81–91. https://doi.org/10.1353/csd.2003.0005.

Janosik, Steven M., and Ellen Plummer. 2005. "The Clery Act, Campus Safety and the Views of Assault Victim Advocates." *College Student Affairs Journal* 25 (1): 116–30. https://eric.ed.gov/?id=EJ957017.

Jenkins, Eric S. 2014. "The Modes of Visual Rhetoric: Circulating Memes as Expressions." *Quarterly Journal of Speech* 100 (4): 442–66. https://doi.org/10.1080/00335630.2014.989258.

Johnson, Davi. 2007. "Mapping the Meme: A Geographical Approach to Materialist Rhetorical Criticism." *Communication and Critical/Cultural Studies* 4 (1): 27–50. https://doi.org/10.1080/14791420601138286.

Johnson, Julia R., Marc Rich, and Aaron Castelan Cargile. 2008. "'Why Are You Shoving This Stuff down Our Throats?': Preparing Intercultural Educators to Challenge Performances of White Racism." *Journal of International & Intercultural Communication* 1 (2): 113–35. https://doi.org/10.1080/17513050801891952.

Johnson, K. C., and Stuart Taylor. 2017. *The Campus Rape Frenzy: The Attack on Due Process at America's Universities.* New York: Encounter Books.

Jozkowski, Kristen N., and Jacquelyn D. Wiersma. 2015. "Does Drinking Alcohol Prior to Sexual Activity Influence College Students' Consent?" *International Journal of Sexual Health* 27 (2): 156–74. https://doi.org/10.1080/19317611.2014.951505.

Jourian, T. J., Symone L. Simmons, and Kara C. Devaney. 2015. "'We Are Not Expected': Trans* Educators (Re)Claiming Space and Voice in Higher Education and Student Affairs." *TSQ: Transgender Studies Quarterly* 2 (3): 431–46. https://doi.org/10.1215/23289252-2926410.

Kafer, Alison. 2013. *Feminist, Queer, Crip.* Bloomington, IN: Indiana University Press.

——. 2016. "Un/Safe Disclosures: Scenes of Disability and Trauma." *Journal of Literary & Cultural Disability Studies* 10 (1): 1–20. https://doi.org/10.1353/jlc.2016.0011.

Kilmartin, Christopher, and Alan D. Berkowitz. 2005. *Sexual Assault in Context: Teaching College Men About Gender.* Mahwah, NJ: Lawrence Erlbaum.

Kipnis, Laura. 2017. *Unwanted Advances: Sexual Paranoia Comes to Campus.* New York: HarperCollins.

Kirkham, Alli. 2015. "What If We Treated All Consent Like Society Treats Sexual Consent?" *Everyday Feminism.* June 23, 2015. https://everydayfeminism.com/2015/06/how-society-treats-consent/

Kiss, Alison, and Kiersten N. Feeney White. 2016. "Looking Beyond the Numbers: Understanding the Jeanne Clery Act and Sexual Violence." In *The Crisis of Campus Sexual Violence: Critical Perspectives on Prevention and Response,* edited by Sara Carrigan Wooten and Roland W. Mitchell, 95–112. New York: Routledge.

Kosenko, Kami, Lance Rintamaki, and Kathleen Maness. 2015. "Patient-Centered Communication: The Experiences of Transgender Adults." In *Transgender*

*Communication Studies: Histories, Trends, and Trajectories*, edited by Leland G. Spencer and Jamie C. Capuzza, 3–17. Lanham, MD: Lexington Books.

Koss, Mary P. 2010. "Restorative Justice for Acquaintance Rape and Misdemeanor Sex Crimes." In *Restorative Justice and Violence Against Women*, edited by James Ptacek, 218–38. Oxford, England: Oxford University Press.

Koss, Mary P., Karen J. Bachar, and C. Quince Hopkins. 2003. "Restorative Justice for Sexual Violence—Repairing Victims, Building Community, and Holding Offenders Accountable." *Annals of the New York Academy of Sciences,* 384–96.

Krivoshey, Mira S., Rachel Adkins, Rebecca Hayes, Julianna M. Nemeth, and Elizabeth G. Klein. 2013. "Sexual Assault Reporting Procedures at Ohio Colleges." *Journal of American College Health* 61 (3): 142–47.

Kronsell, Annica and Erika Svedberg, eds. 2012. *Making Gender, Making War: Violence, Military and Peacekeeping Practices.* New York: Routledge.

Kulbaga, Theresa A. 2008. "Pleasurable Pedagogies: *Reading Lolita in Tehran* and the Rhetoric of Empathy." *College English* 70 (5): 506–21.

—. 2016. "Sari Suasion: Migrant Economies of Care in Shailja Patel's *Migritude*." *Prose Studies* 38 (1): 74–92.

Kulbaga, Theresa A., and Leland G. Spencer. 2017. "Fitness and the Feminist First Lady: Gender, Race, and Body in Michelle Obama's *Let's Move!* Campaign." *Women & Language* 40 (1): 36–50.

Kuznekoff, Jeffrey H., Leland G. Spencer, and Robert N. Burt. 2017. "Online Communication Regarding Ohio's 2016 Presidential Primary." In *The Presidency and Social Media: Discourse, Disruption, and Digital Democracy in the 2016 Presidential Election*, edited by Dan Schill and John Allen Hendricks, 72–89. New York: Routledge.

Lakämper, Judith. 2017. "Affective Dissonance, Neoliberal Postfeminism and the Foreclosure of Solidarity." *Feminist Theory* 18 (2):119–35. https://doi.org/10.1177/1464700117700041.

Laker, Jason, and Erica Boas. 2017. *Consent Stories.* http://www.consentstories.org/.

Larabee, Ann. 2018. "Celebrity, Politics, and the 'Me, Too' Movement." *Journal of Popular Culture* 51 (1): 7–9. https://doi.org/10.1111/jpcu.12650

Laymon, Kiese. 2018. *Heavy: An American Memoir.* New York: Simon and Schuster.

LeBlanc, Stephanie, and Elizabeth Anne Kinsella. 2016. "Toward Epistemic Justice: A Critically Reflexive Examination of 'Sanism' and Implications for Knowledge Generation." *Studies in Social Justice* 10 (1): 59–78. https://doi.org/10.26522/ssj.v10i1.1324.

Lehr, Jennifer. 2017. *ParentSpeak: What's Wrong with How We Talk to Our Children—and What to Say Instead.* New York: Workman Publishing.

Lerner, Gerda. 1986. *The Creation of Patriarchy.* New York: Oxford University Press.

Lockhart, Eleanor Amaranth. 2016. "Why Trigger Warnings Are Beneficial,

Perhaps Even Necessary." *First Amendment Studies* 50 (2): 59–69. https://doi.org/10.1080/21689725.2016.1232623.

Loofbourow, Lili. 2018. "Junot Díaz and the Problem of the Male Self-Pardon." *Slate.* 24 June. https://slate.com/culture/2018/06/junot-diaz-allegations-and-the-male-self-pardon.html.

Lorde, Audre. 1984. *Sister Outsider: Essays and Speeches.* New York: Ten Speed Press.

Lukianoff, Greg, and Jonathan Haidt. 2015. "The Coddling of the American Mind." *The Atlantic.* https://www.theatlantic.com/magazine/archive/2015/09/the-coddling-of-the-american-mind/399356/.

Lynch, Maggie McVay. 2002. *The Online Educator: A Guide to Creating the Virtual Classroom.* New York: Routledge.

MacKinnon, Catherine. 1983. "Feminism, Marxism, Method, and the State: Toward Feminist Jurisprudence." *Signs* 8.4 (Summer): 635–58.

Maddux, Kristy. 2009. "Winning the Right to Vote in 2004." *Feminist Media Studies* 9 (1): 73–94. https://doi.org/10.1080/14680770802619516.

Mailhot, Terese Marie. 2018. *Heart Berries: A Memoir.* Berkeley: Counterpoint.

Malatino, Hilary. 2015. "Pedagogies of Becoming: Trans Inclusivity and the Crafting of Being." *TSQ: Transgender Studies Quarterly* 2 (3): 395–410. https://doi.org/10.1215/23289252-2926387.

Manne, Kate. 2018. *Down Girl: The Logic of Misogyny.* New York: Oxford University Press.

Manne, Kate, and Jason Stanley. 2015. "When Free Speech Becomes a Political Weapon." *The Chronicle of Higher Education.* November 13, 2015. https://www.chronicle.com/article/When-Free-Speech-Becomes-a/234207.

Manning, Jimmie, and Adrianne Kunkel. 2013. *Researching Interpersonal Relationships: Qualitative Methods, Studies, and Analysis.* Thousand Oaks, CA: SAGE.

Marine, Susan B., and Z Nicolazzo. 2017. "Campus Sexual Violence Prevention Educators' Use of Gender in Their Work: A Critical Exploration." *Journal of Interpersonal Violence.* https://doi.org/10.1177/0886260517718543.

May, Emmaline, and Blue Seat Studios. 2015. "Consent: It's Simple As Tea." https://vimeo.com/126553913.

McGregor, Jena. 2016. "To improve diversity, don't make people go to diversity training. Seriously." *The Washington Post.* July 1, 2016. https://www.washingtonpost.com/news/on-leadership/wp/2016/07/01/to-improve-diversity-dont-make-people-go-to-diversity-training-really-2/.

McGuire, Danielle L. 2010. *At the Dark End of the Street: Black Women, Rape, and Resistance—A New History of the Civil Rights Movement from Rosa Parks to the Rise of Black Power.* New York: Alfred A. Knopf.

McPhail, Beverly A. 2016. "Feminist Framework Plus: Knitting Feminist Theories of Rape Etiology Into a Comprehensive Model." *Trauma, Violence, & Abuse* 17 (3): 314–29. https://doi.org/10.1177/1524838015584367.

McRobbie, Angela. 2004. "Post-Feminism and Popular Culture." *Feminist Media Studies* 4 (3): 255–64.

Melamed, Jodi. 2006. "The Spirit of Neoliberalism: From Racial Liberalism to Neoliberal Multiculturalism." *Social Text* 24 (4): 1–24. https://doi.org/ 10.1215/01642472-2006-009.

Mental Health Association of Maryland, Missouri Department of Mental Health, and National Council for Behavioral Health. 2013. *Mental Health First Aid USA.* Revised 1st ed. Lutherville, MD: Mental Health Association of Maryland.

Miller, Lucy J. 2015. "Disciplining the Transgender Body: Transgender Microaggressions in a Transitional Era." In *Gender in a Transitional Era: Changes and Challenges*, edited by Amanda R. Martinez and Lucy J. Miller, 133–50. Lanham, MD: Lexington Books.

Millett, Kate. 1970. *Sexual Politics.* New York: Columbia University Press.

Mock, Janet. 2014. *Redefining Realness: My Path to Womanhood, Identity, Love, and So Much More.* New York: Atria Paperback.

Mohanty, Chandra Talpade. 2013. "Transnational Feminist Crossings: On Neoliberalism and Radical Critique." *Signs* 38 (4): 967–91.

Moncrief, Stephen. 2017. "Military Socialization, Disciplinary Culture, and Sexual Violence in UN Peacekeeping Operations." *Journal of Peace Research* 54 (5): 715–30. https://doi.org/10.1177/0022343317716784.

Mone, Mark. 2016. "Chancellor's Update: UWM Stands Together." December 13, 2016. http://uwm.edu/chancellor/chancellors-update-uwm-stands-together/.

Moore, Anne Elizabeth. 2017. *Body Horror: Capitalism, Fear, Misogyny, Jokes.* Chicago: Curbside Splendor Publishing.

Moraga, Cherríe. *Loving in the War Years: Lo Que Nunca Paso por Sus Labios.* San Francisco: Aunt Lute Books.

Moraga, Cherríe, and Gloria Anzaldúa. 1981. *This Bridge Called My Back: Writings by Radical Women of Color.* 4th ed. Albany: SUNY Press.

Morgan, Robin, ed. 1970. *Sisterhood is Powerful: An Anthology of Writings from the Women's Liberation Movement.* New York: Vintage Books.

Morrison, Toni. 1970. *The Bluest Eye.* New York: Holt, Rinehart, and Winston.

Murphy, Amy, and Brian Van Brunt. 2017. *Uprooting Sexual Violence in Higher Education: A Guide for Practitioners and Faculty.* New York: Routledge.

MVP Strategies: Mentors in Violence Prevention. 2015. https://www.mvpstrat.com/.

Nagel, Joane. 2014. "Plus ça Change: Reflections on a Century of Militarizing Women's Sexuality." *European Journal of Women's Studies* 21.3 (August): 294–300.

National Center on Domestic and Sexual Violence. 2017. Power and Control Wheel. http://www.ncdsv.org/images/PowerControlwheelNOSHADING.pdf.

National Center on Universal Design for Learning. 2015. http://www.udlcenter.org/

National Sexual Violence Resource Center (NSVRC). 2015. "Statistics About

Sexual Violence." http://www.nsvrc.org/sites/default/files/publications_nsvrc_factsheet_media-packet_statistics-about-sexual-violence_0.pdf.

National Union of Students. 2016. "Sexual Consent—is not like tea." 27 April. https://www.nusconnect.org.uk/articles/sexual-consent-is-not-like-tea.

Neville, Patricia. 2012. "Helping Self-Help Books: Working Towards a New Research Agenda." *Interactions: Studies in Communication & Culture* 3(3): 361–79. https://doi.org/10.1386/iscc.3.3.361_1.

Nicolazzo, Z. 2015. "'Just Go In Looking Good': The Resilience, Resistance, and Kinship-Building of Trans* College Students." Miami University. https://etd.ohiolink.edu/ap/10?0::NO:10:P10_ACCESSION_NUM: miami1426251164.

———. 2016. *Trans* in College: Transgender Students' Strategies for Navigating Campus Life and the Institutional Politics of Inclusion*. Sterling, Virginia: Stylus Publishing.

Nova News Now. 2017. "Acadia football players seek to prevent violence." Nova News Now.com. Last modified September 30, 2017. https://www.novanewsnow.com/living/acadia-football-players-seek-to-prevent-violence-72041/.

Novkov, Julie. 2016. "Equality, Process, and Campus Sexual Assault." *Maryland Law Review* 75: 590–619.

O'Brien Hallstein, D. Lynn. 1999. "A Postmodern Caring: Feminist Standpoint Theories, Revisioned Caring, and Communication Ethics." *Western Journal of Communication* 63 (1): 32–56.

Odello, Marco, and Róisín Burke. 2016. "Between immunity and impunity: peacekeeping and sexual abuses and violence." *International Journal of Human Rights* 20.6 (August): 839–53. https://doi.org/10.1080/13642987. 2016.1176810.

O'Dowd, Peter. 2016. "University of Chicago Tells Freshmen: Don't Expect Trigger Warnings, Safe Spaces." *Here & Now*. August 26, 2016. https://www.wbur.org/hereandnow/2016/08/26/uchicago-trigger-warnings.

Ohio Alliance to End Sexual Violence (OAESV). 2012. "Sexual Assault in Ohio: Fact Sheet of Legal Definitions." https://www.publicsafety.ohio.gov/links/ocjs_Sexual_Assault_2013.pdf.

Oliver, Kelly. 2015. "Party Rape, Nonconsensual Sex, and Affirmative Consent Policies." *Americana : The Journal of American Popular Culture, 1900 to Present* 14 (2). http://www.americanpopularculture.com/journal/articles/fall_2015/ oliver.htm.

———. 2016. Hunting Girls: Sexual Violence from "The Hunger Games" to Campus Rape. New York: Columbia University Press.

O'Reilley, Mary Rose. 1993. The Peaceable Classroom. Portsmouth, NH: Heinemann.

———. 1998. Radical Presence: Teaching as Contemplative Practice. Portsmouth,

NH: Boynton/Cook Publishers, Inc. Overpass Light Brigade. 2016. "Hate's Insidious Face: UW-Milwaukee and the
'Alt-Right.'" December 14, 2016. http://overpasslightbrigade.org/hates-insidious-face-uw-milwaukee-and-the-alt-right/.

Owen, A. Susan. 1999. "Vampires, Postmodernity, and Postfeminism: *Buffy the Vampire Slayer.*" *Journal of Popular Film and Television* 27 (2): 24–31. https://doi.org/10.1080/01956059909602801.

Patel, Shailja. 2010. *Migritude.* Los Angeles: Kaya Press.

Patil, Vrushali, Bandana Purkayastha, Vrushali Patil, and Bandana Purkayastha. 2015. "Sexual Violence, Race and Media (In)Visibility: Intersectional Complexities in a Transnational Frame." *Societies* 5 (3): 598–617. https://doi.org/10.3390/soc5030598.

Patterson, G. 2016. "The Unbearable Weight of Pedagogical Neutrality: Religion and LGBTQ Issues in the English Studies Classroom." In *Sexual Rhetorics: Methods, Identities, Publics*, edited by Jonathan Alexander and Jacqueline Rhodes, 134–46. New York: Routledge.

——. 2018. "Entertaining a Healthy Cispicion of the Ally Industrial Complex in Transgender Studies." *Women & Language* 41 (1): 146–51.

Patterson, G, and Leland G. Spencer. 2017. "What's So Funny about a Snowman in a Tiara? Exploring Gender Identity and Gender Nonconformity in Children's Animated Films." *Queer Studies in Media & Popular Culture* 2 (1): 73–93.

Pérez, Miriam Zoila. 2008. "When Sexual Autonomy Isn't Enough: Sexual Violence Against Immigrant Women in the United States." *Yes Means Yes: Visions of Female Sexual Power and a World Without Rape.* Edited by Jaclyn Friedman and Jessica Valenti. Berkeley: Seal Press.

Pharr, Suzanne. 2014. "Homophobia as a Weapon of Sexism." In *Race, Class, and Gender in the United States*, edited by Paula S. Rothenberg and Kelly S. Mayhew, 9th ed., 163–72. New York: Worth.

Pina, Afroditi, Theresa A. Gannon, and Benjamin Saunders. 2009. "An Overview of the Literature on Sexual Harassment: Perpetrator, Theory, and Treatment Issues." *Aggression and Violent Behavior* 14 (2): 126–38. https://doi.org/10.1016/j.avb.2009.01.002.

Pino, Andrea. 2016. "A Note on Representation." In *We Believe You: Survivors of Campus Sexual Assault Speak Out*, Annie E. Clark and Andrea L. Pino. New York: Holt Paperbacks.

Platero, Raquel Lucas, and Em Harsin Drager. 2015. "Two Trans* Teachers in Madrid: Interrogating Trans*formative Pedagogies." *TSQ: Transgender Studies Quarterly* 2 (3): 447–63. https://doi.org/10.1215/23289252-2926419.

Pohlhaus, Gaile, Jr. 2011. "Relational Knowing and Epistemic Injustice: Toward a Theory of Willful Hermeneutical Ignorance." *Hypatia* 27 (4): 715–735. https://doi.org/10.1111/j.1527-2001.2011.01222.x.

———. 2014. "Discerning the Primary Epistemic Harm in Cases of Testimonial Injustice." *Social Epistemology* 28 (2): 99–114. https://doi.org/10.1080/026917 28.2013.782581.

Posadas, Jeremy. 2017. "Teaching the Cause of Rape Culture: Toxic Masculinity." *Journal of Feminist Studies in Religion* 33 (1):177–79. https://doi.org/ 10.2979/jfemistudreli.33.1.23.

Rae, Logan. 2016. "Re-Focusing the Debate on Trigger Warnings: Privilege, Trauma, and Disability in the Classroom." *First Amendment Studies* 50 (2): 95–102. https://doi.org/10.1080/21689725.2016.1224677.

Rape, Abuse, and Incest National Network (RAINN). 2018. "Victims of Sexual Violence: Statistics." https://www.rainn.org/statistics/victims-sexual-violence.

Rich, Marc D., Ebony A. Utley, Kelly Janke, and Minodora Moldoveanu. 2010. "'I'd Rather Be Doing Something Else:' Male Resistance to Rape Prevention Programs." *The Journal of Men's Studies* 18 (3): 268–88. https://doi. org/10.3149/jms.1803.268.

Richards, Tara N., Kathryn A. Branch, Ruth E. Fleury-Steiner, and Katherine Kafonek. 2017. "A Feminist Analysis of Campus Sexual Assault Policies: Results from a National Sample." *Family Relations* 66 (1): 104–15. https://doi. org/10.1111/fare.12236

Roberts, John Michael. 2014. *New Media and Public Activism: Neoliberalism, the State and Radical Protest in the Public Sphere*. Bristol, UK: Policy Press.

RockstarDinosaurPiratePrincess. 2015. "Consent: Not Actually That Complicated." March 2. http://rockstardinosaurpirateprincess.com/2015/03/02/consent-not-actually-that-complicated/.

Rood, Craig. 2013. "Rhetorics of Civility: Theory, Pedagogy, and Practice in Speaking and Writing Textbooks." *Rhetoric Review* 32 (3): 331–48. https://doi.org/10.1080/07350198.2013.797879.

———. 2014. "'Moves' toward Rhetorical Civility." *Pedagogy: Critical Approaches to Teaching Literature Language Composition and Culture* 14 (3): 395–415. https://doi.org/10.1215/15314200-2715778.

Rozee, Patricia D., and Mary P. Koss. 2001. "Rape: A Century of Resistance." *Psychology of Women Quarterly* 25 (4): 295–311. https://doi.org/ 10.1111/1471-6402.00030.

Salter, Michael. 2013. "Justice and Revenge in Online Counter-Publics: Emerging Responses to Sexual Violence in the Age of Social Media." *Crime, Media, Culture* 9 (3): 225–42. https://doi.org/10.1177/1741659013493918.

Sarkeesian, Anita, and Katherine Cross. 2015. "Your Humanity Is in Another Castle: Terror Dreams and the Harassment of Women." In *The State of Play: Creators and Critics on Video Game Culture*, edited by Daniel Goldberg and Linus Larsson, 103–26. New York: Seven Stories Press.

Saul, Stephanie, and Kate Taylor. 2017. "Betsy DeVos Reverses Obama-Era Policy on Campus Sexual Assault Investigations." September 22, 2017. https://www.nytimes.com/2017/09/22/us/devos-colleges-sex-assault.html.

SAVE. 2010. "Don't Be That Guy Pt. 1." *Sexual Assault Voices of Edmonton.* https://www.savedmonton.com/dont-be-that-guy-1.html.

——. 2012. "Don't Be That Guy Pt. 2." *Sexual Assault Voices of Edmonton.* http://www.SAVEdmonton.com/dont-be-that-guy-2.html.

Scott, Joan W. 2001. "The Evidence of Experience." *Critical Inquiry* 17 (4): 773–97.

Scott, Karla D. 2013. "Communication Strategies across Cultural Borders: Dispelling Stereotypes, Performing Competence, and Redefining Black Womanhood." *Women's Studies in Communication* 36 (3): 312–29. https://doi.org/10.1080/07491409.2013.831005.

Shaw, Lori E. 2016. "Title IX, Sexual Assault, and the Issue of Effective Consent: Blurred Lines—When Should 'Yes' Mean 'No'?" *Indiana Law Journal* 91: 1363–423.

Shifman, Limor. 2013. "Memes in a Digital World: Reconciling with a Conceptual Troublemaker." *Journal of Computer-Mediated Communication* 18 (3): 362–77. https://doi.org/10.1111/jcc4.12013.

——. 2014. *Memes in Digital Culture.* Cambridge, MA: MIT Press.

Shreerekha. 2018. "In the Wake of His Damage." *The Rumpus.* May 12, 2018. https://therumpus.net/2018/05/in-the-wake-of-his-damage/.

Sills, Sophie, Chelsea Pickens, Karishma Beach, Lloyd Jones, Octavia Calder-Dawe, Paulette Benton-Greig, and Nicola Gavey. 2016. "Rape Culture and Social Media: Young Critics and a Feminist Counterpublic." *Feminist Media Studies* 16 (6): 935–51. https://doi.org/10.1080/14680777.2015.1137962.

Simi, Olivera. 2010. "Does the Presence of Women Really Matter? Towards Combating Male Sexual Violence in Peacekeeping Operations." *International Peacekeeping* 17 (2): 188–99. https://doi.org/10.1080/13533311003625084.

Skjelsbæk, Inger. 2007. "Sexual Violence in Times of War: A New Challenge for Peace Operations?" *International Peacekeeping* 8 (2): 69–84. https://doi.org/10.1080/13533310108413896.

Solnit, Rebecca. 2014. *Men Explain Things To Me.* Chicago: Haymarket Books.

——. 2016. "The Case of the Missing Perpetrator: On Mysterious Pregnancies, the Passive Voice, and Disappearing Men." *Literary Hub.* February 11, 2016. http://lithub.com/rebecca-solnit-the-case-of-the-missing-perpetrator/.

Spencer, Leland G. 2013. "Presiding Bishop Katharine Jefferts Schori and Possibilities for a Progressive Civility." *Southern Communication Journal* 78 (5): 447–65. https://doi.org/10.1080/1041794X.2013.847480.

——. 2014. "Performing Transgender Identity in *The Little Mermaid*: From Andersen to Disney." *Communication Studies* 65 (1): 112–27. https://doi.org/10.1080/10510974.2013.832691.

—. 2015a. "Engaging Undergraduates in Feminist Classrooms: An Exploration of Professors' Practices." *Equity & Excellence in Education* 48 (2): 195–211. https://doi.org/10.1080/10665684.2015.1022909.

—. 2015b. "Introduction: Centering Transgender Studies and Gender Identity in Communication Scholarship." In *Transgender Communication Studies: Histories, Trends, and Trajectories,* edited by Leland G. Spencer and Jamie C. Capuzza, ix–xxii. Lanham, MD: Lexington Books.

—. 2017. *Women Bishops and Rhetorics of Shalom: A Whole Peace.* Lanham, MD: Lexington Books.

Spencer, Leland G., and Joshua Trey Barnett. 2011. "When Men Are Sexually Harassed: A Foundation for Studying Men's Experiences as Targets of Sexual Harassment." *Speaker & Gavel* 48 (2): 53–67.

Spencer, Leland G., and Jamie Capuzza. 2016. "Centering Gender Identity and Transgender Lives in Instructional Communication Research." *Communication Education* 65 (1): 113–17. https://doi.org/10.1080/03634523.2015.1096949.

Spencer, Leland G., and G Patterson. 2017. "Abridging the Acronym: Neoliberalism and the Proliferation of Identitarian Politics." *Journal of LGBT Youth* 14 (3): 296–316. https://doi.org/10.1080/19361653.2017.1324343.

Spencer, Leland G., Pamela M. Tyahur, and Jennifer A. Jackson. 2016. "Civility and Academic Freedom: Extending the Conversation." *Journal of Contemporary Rhetoric* 6 (3/4): 50–61.

Sprankles, Julie. 2016. "8 Brock Turner Headlines That Totally Miss The Point." *Bustle.* June 6, 2016. https://www.bustle.com/articles/165164-8-brock-turner-headlines-that-totally-miss-the-point.

Springer, Simon. 2016. "Fuck Neoliberalism." *ACME: An International Journal for Critical Geographies* 15 (2): 285–92.

Spry, Tami. 1995. "In the Absence of Word and Body: Hegemonic Implications of 'Victim' and 'Survivor' in Women's Narratives of Sexual Violence." *Women & Language* 13 (2): 27–32.

Stanley, Jason. 2016. "The Free-Speech Fallacy." *The Chronicle of Higher Education* February 26, 2016. https://www.chronicle.com/article/The-Free-Speech-Fallacy/235520.

Step UP! Program. 2018. "Step UP!" http://stepupprogram.org/.

Stotzer, Rebecca L. 2009. "Violence against Transgender People: A Review of United States Data." *Aggression and Violent Behavior* 14 (3): 170–79. https://doi.org/10.1016/j.avb.2009.01.006.

Strasser, Annie-Rose, and Tara Culp-Ressler. 2013. "How The Media Took Sides In The Steubenville Rape Case." *ThinkProgress* (blog). March 18, 2013. https://thinkprogress.org/how-the-media-took-sides-in-the-steubenville-rape-case-e92589afbadf/.Stringer, Rebecca. 2014. *Knowing Victims: Feminism, Agency and Victim Politics in Neoliberal Times.* New York: Routledge.

—. 2016. "Trigger Warnings in University Teaching." *Women's Studies Journal* 30 (2): 62–66.

Tasker, Yvonne, and Diane Negra, eds. 2007. *Interrogating Postfeminism: Gender and the Politics of Popular Culture.* Durham, NC: Duke University Press.

Tharp, Andra Teten, Sarah DeGue, Karen Lang, Linda Anne Valle, Greta Massetti, Melissa Holt, and Jennifer Matjasko. 2011. "Commentary on Foubert, Godin, & Tatum (2010): The Evolution of Sexual Violence Prevention and the Urgency for Effectiveness." *Journal of Interpersonal Violence* 26 (16): 3383–92. https://doi.org/10.1177/0886260510393010.

Thorpe, M. Elizabeth. 2016. "Trigger Warnings, the Organic Classroom, and Civil Discourse." *First Amendment Studies* 50 (2): 83–94. https://doi.org/10.1080/21689725.2016.1219270.

Tolentino, Jia. 2018. "The Rising Pressure of the #MeToo Backlash." *The New Yorker.* January 24, 2018. https://www.newyorker.com/culture/culture-desk/the-rising-pressure-of-the-metoo-backlash.

Troost, Hazel/Cedar. 2008. "Reclaiming Touch: Rape Culture, Explicit Verbal Consent, and Body Sovereignty." In *Yes Means Yes!: Visions of Female Sexual Power and a World Without Rape*, edited by Jaclyn Friedman and Jessica Valenti, 171–78. Berkeley: Seal Press.

Trujillo, Nick. 1991. "Hegemonic Masculinity on the Mound: Media Representations of Nolan Ryan and American Sports Culture." *Critical Studies in Mass Communication* 8 (3): 290–308.

Tuerkheimer, Deborah. 2015. "Rape on and off Campus." *Emory Law Journal* 65: 1–45.

United Nations Population Fund. 2017. "Gender-Based Violence." https://www.unfpa.org/publications.

U.S. Department of Education. 2017. "Department of Education Issues New Interim Guidance on Campus Sexual Misconduct." September 22, 2017. https://www.ed.gov/news/press-releases/department-education-issues-new-interim-guidance-campus-sexual-misconduct.

U.S. Department of Justice. 2000. *Full Report of the Prevalence, Incidence, and Consequences of Violence Against Women: Findings from the National Violence Against Women Survey.* https://www.ncjrs.gov/pdffiles1/nij/183781.pdf.

U.S. Department of Justice, Bureau of Justice Statistics. 2014. "Rape and Sexual Assault Victimization Among College-Age Females, 1995–2013." https://www.bjs.gov/content/pub/pdf/rsavcaf9513.pdf.

Valenti, Jessica. 2014. "'Yes means yes' laws will not actually reclassify all sex at universities as rape." *The Guardian.* October 7, 2014. https://www.theguardian.com/commentisfree/2014/oct/07/yes-means-yes-sex-rape-universities.

Vatz, Richard E. 2016. "The Academically Destructive Nature of Trigger

Warnings." *First Amendment Studies* 50 (2): 51–58. https://doi.org/10.1080/21 689725.2016.1230508.

Vendantam, Shankar. 2008. "Most Diversity Training Ineffective, Study Finds." January 20. http://www.washingtonpost.com/wp-dyn/content/article/2008/01/19/AR2008011901899.html.

Wagner, Anne, and Jamie Lynn Magnusson. 2005. "Neglected Realities: Exploring the Impact of Women's Experiences of Violence on Learning in Sites of Higher Education." *Gender & Education* 17 (4): 449–61.

Wagner, Cathy, Theresa Kulbaga, and Jennifer Cohen. 2017. "Imperial Partitioning in the Neoliberal University." *World Social and Economic Review* 2017: 61–78.

Warner, Michael. 2000. *The Trouble with Normal: Sex, Politics, and the Ethics of Queer Life*. Cambridge, MA: Harvard University Press.

Weiss, Suzannah. 2016. "5 Things We're Not Taught to Get Consent For, But Should Be." *Bustle*. September 6, 2016. https://www.bustle.com/articles/182508-5-things-were-not-taught-to-get-consent-for-but-should-be.

West, Robin L. 1993. "Legitimizing the Illegitimate: A Comment on *Beyond Rape*." *Columbia Law Review* 93: 1442–59.

Willis, Ellen. 1982. "Toward a Feminist Sexual Revolution." *Social Text* 6 (Autumn): 3–21. https://doi.org/10.2307/466614.

Winterich, Julie. 2016. "Emerging Feminisms, If College Heterosexual, Cis Men Were Raped More Than Everyone Else." *The Feminist Wire*. April 7, 2016. http://www.thefeministwire.com/2016/04/if-college-heterosexual-cis-men-were-raped-more-than-everyone-else.

Wood, Julia T. 1995. "Feminist Scholarship and the Study of Relationships." *Journal of Social and Personal Relationships* 12 (1): 103–20. https://doi.org/10.1177/0265407595121007.

——. 2011. *Gendered Lives: Communication, Gender, and Culture*. 9th ed. Boston: Wadsworth.

Wyatt, Wendy. 2016. "The Ethics of Trigger Warnings." *Teaching Ethics* 16 (1): 17–35. https://doi.org/10.5840/tej201632427.

Wyss, Shannon E. 2004. "'This Was My Hell': The Violence Experienced by Gender Non-Conforming Youth in US High Schools." *International Journal of Qualitative Studies in Education* 17 (5): 709–30. https://doi.org/10.1080/0951839042000253676.

Ybarra, Michele L. and Kimberly J. Mitchell. 2013. "Prevalence Rates of Male and Female Sexual Violence Perpetrators in a National Sample of Adolescents." *JAMA Pediatrics* 167 (12): 1125–34. https://doi.org/10.1001/jamapediatrics.2013.2629.

Young, Cathy. 2015. "Consent: It's a Piece of Cake." *Spiked*. November 2, 2015.

http://www.spiked-online.com/newsite/article/consent-its-a-piece-of-cake/
17594#.WWE-9RPyu8X.

Zacharek, Stephanie, Eliana Dockterman, and Haley Sweetland Edwards. 2017.
"The Silence Breakers." *Time.* http://time.com/time-person-of-the-year-
2017-silence-breakers/.

Zarefsky, David. 2004. "Presidential Rhetoric and the Power of Definition."
*Presidential Studies Quarterly* 34 (3): 607–19. https://doi.org/10.1111/j.1741--
5705.2004.00214.x.

Zúñiga, Ximena. 2013. "Introduction." In *Readings for Diversity and Social Justice*,
edited by Maurianne Adams, Warren J. Blumenfeld, Carmelita Castañeda,
Heather W. Hackman, Madeline L. Peters, and Ximena Zúñiga, 589–93.
New York: Routledge.

# INDEX